To all the children who embark on this colorful journey through the pages of this book, may your dreams soar high and your imaginations be as vast as the universe. May every stroke, every color and every moment of creation inspire a sparkle in your eyes and a smile on your face. Let this book be an invitation to explore the world of art and creativity. With affection, Tati.

Tatiana Araujo
2024

This Book Belongs to:

T.A.©
all rights reserved

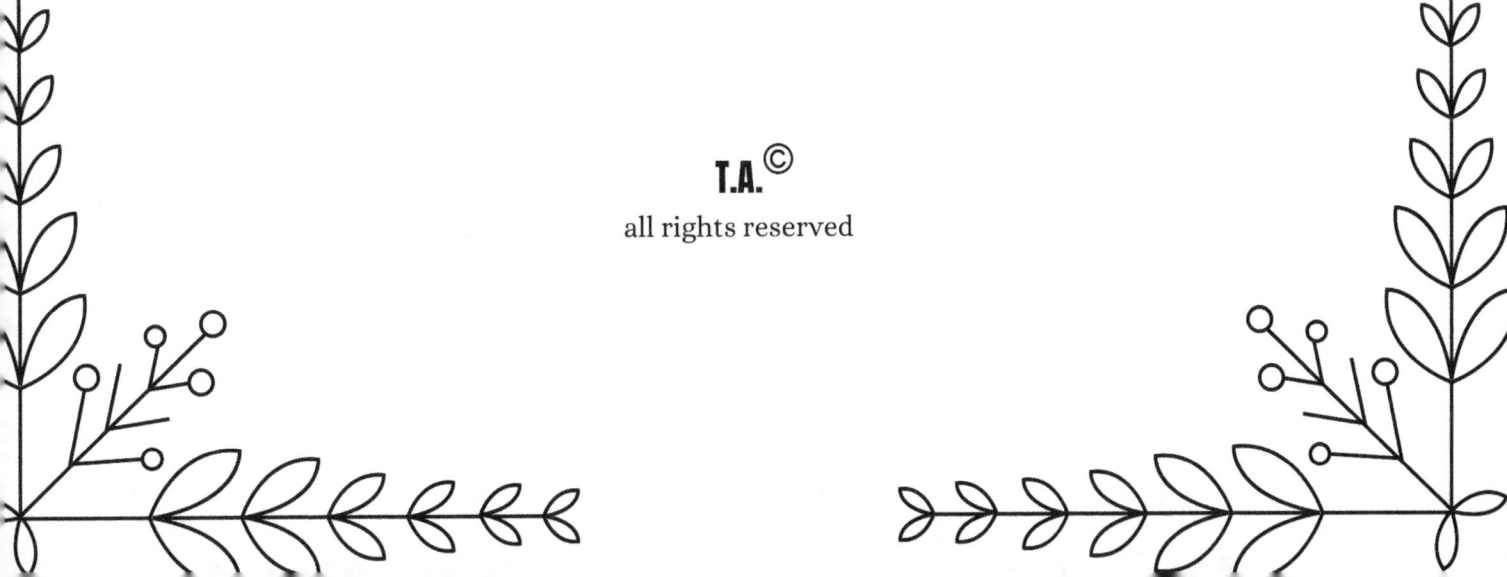

ALL RIGHTS RESERVED
2024

No part of this publication may be reproduced, distributed, or transmitted in any form or by any means, including photocopying, recording, or other electronic or mechanical methods, without the prior written permission of the publisher, except for brief quotations incorporated in critical reviews and other specific noncommercial uses. Any unauthorized replica of this work is prohibited.

T.A.©
Tati Araujo Publications

Color Test Page

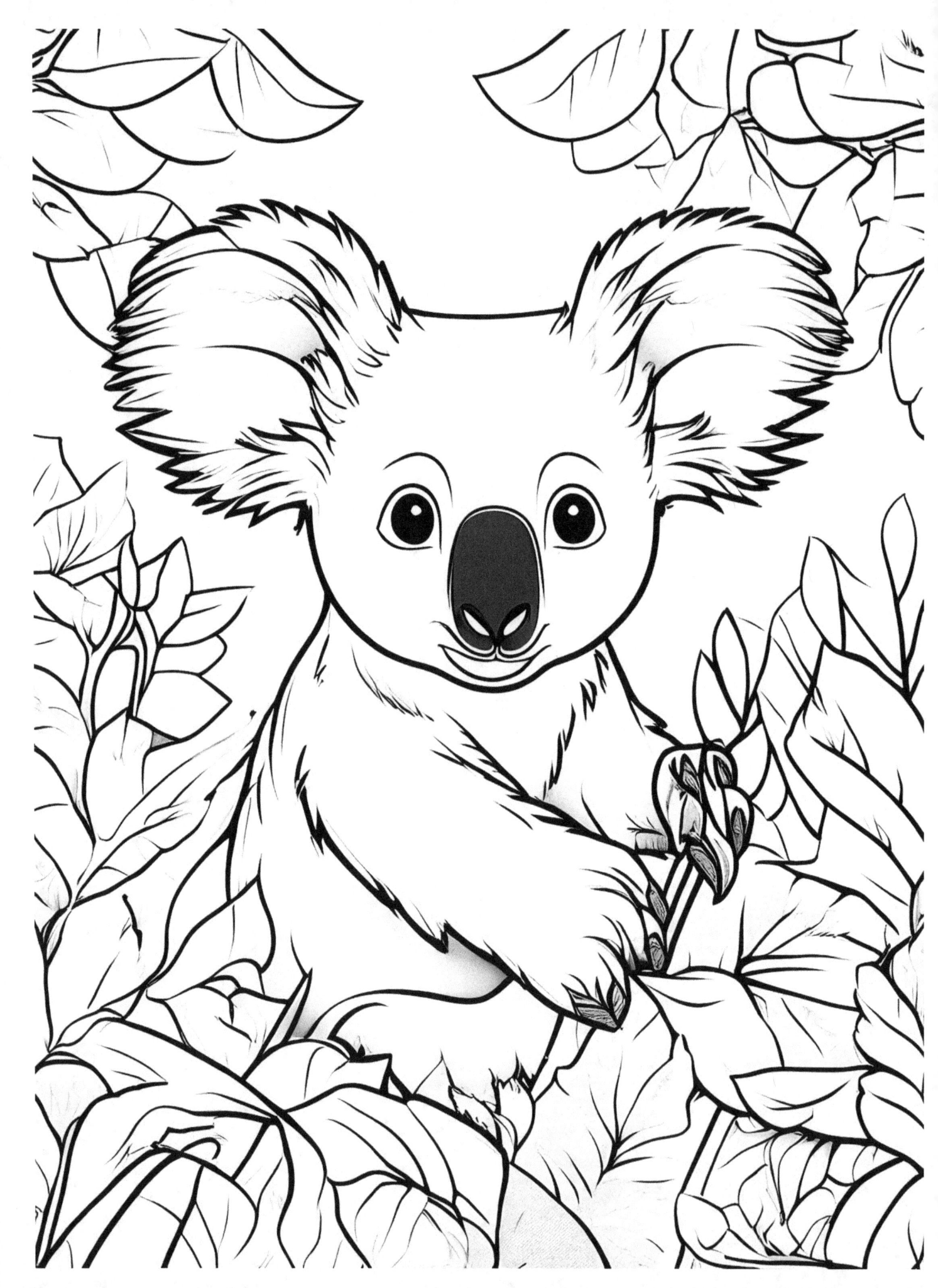

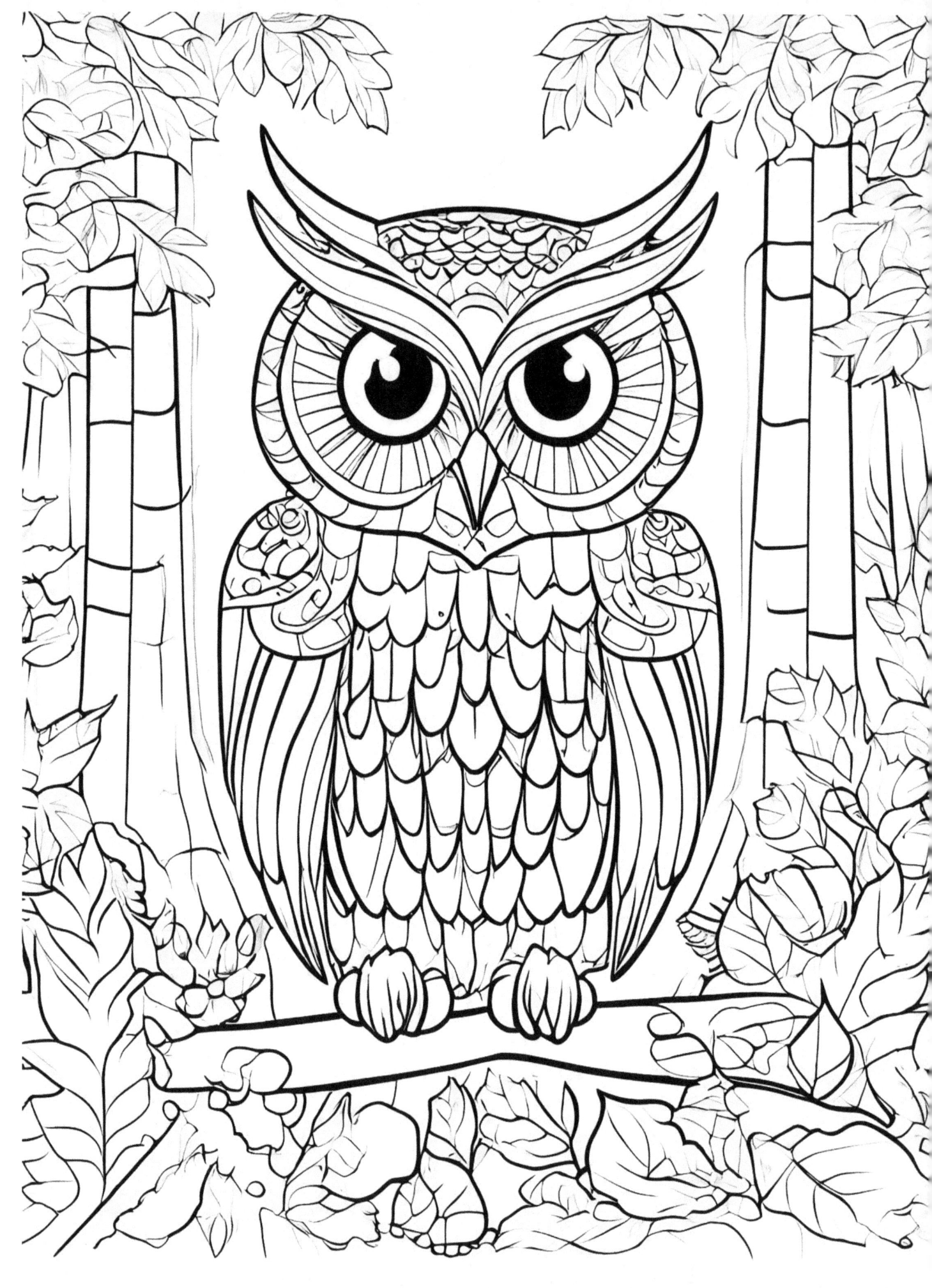

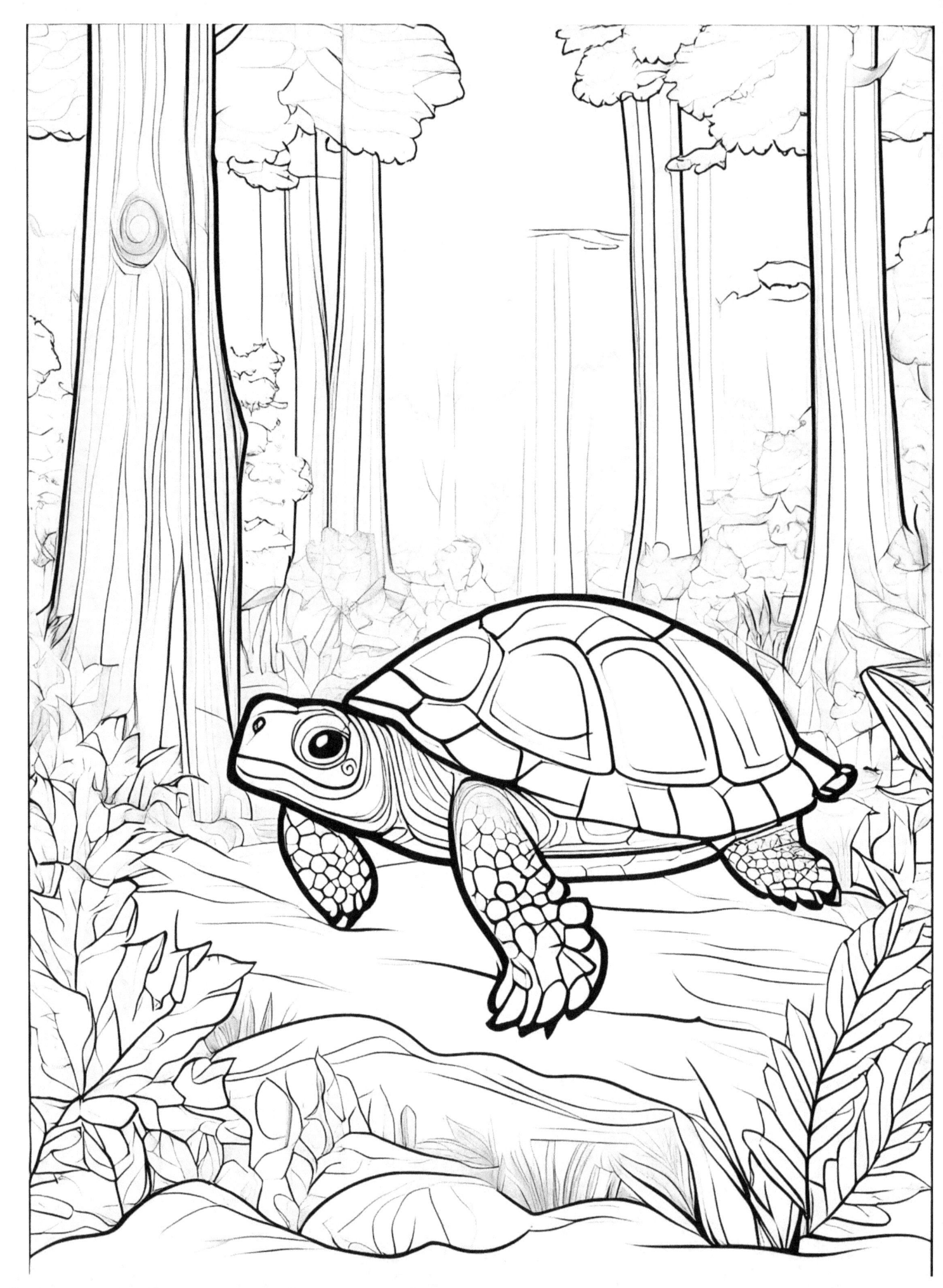

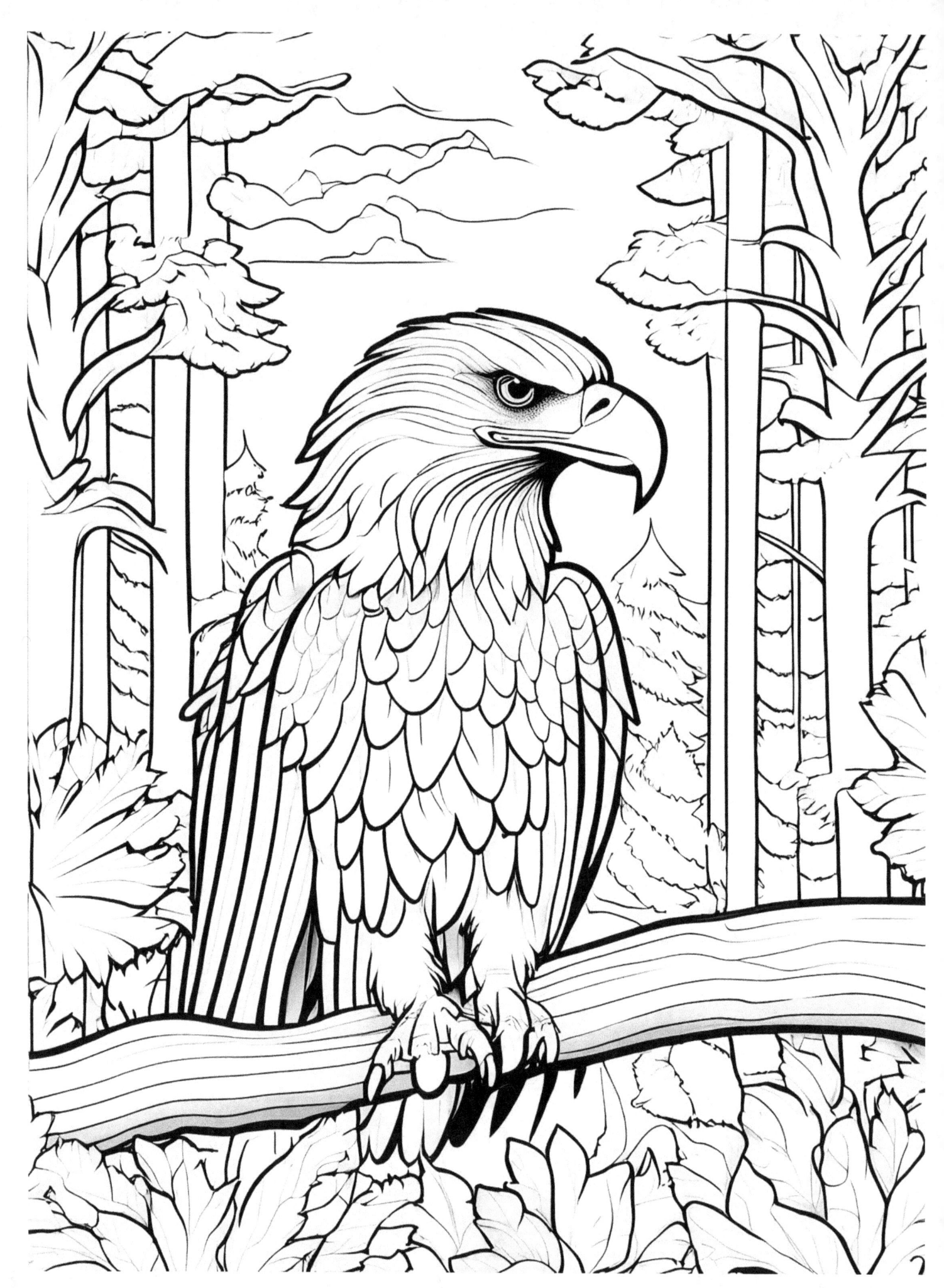

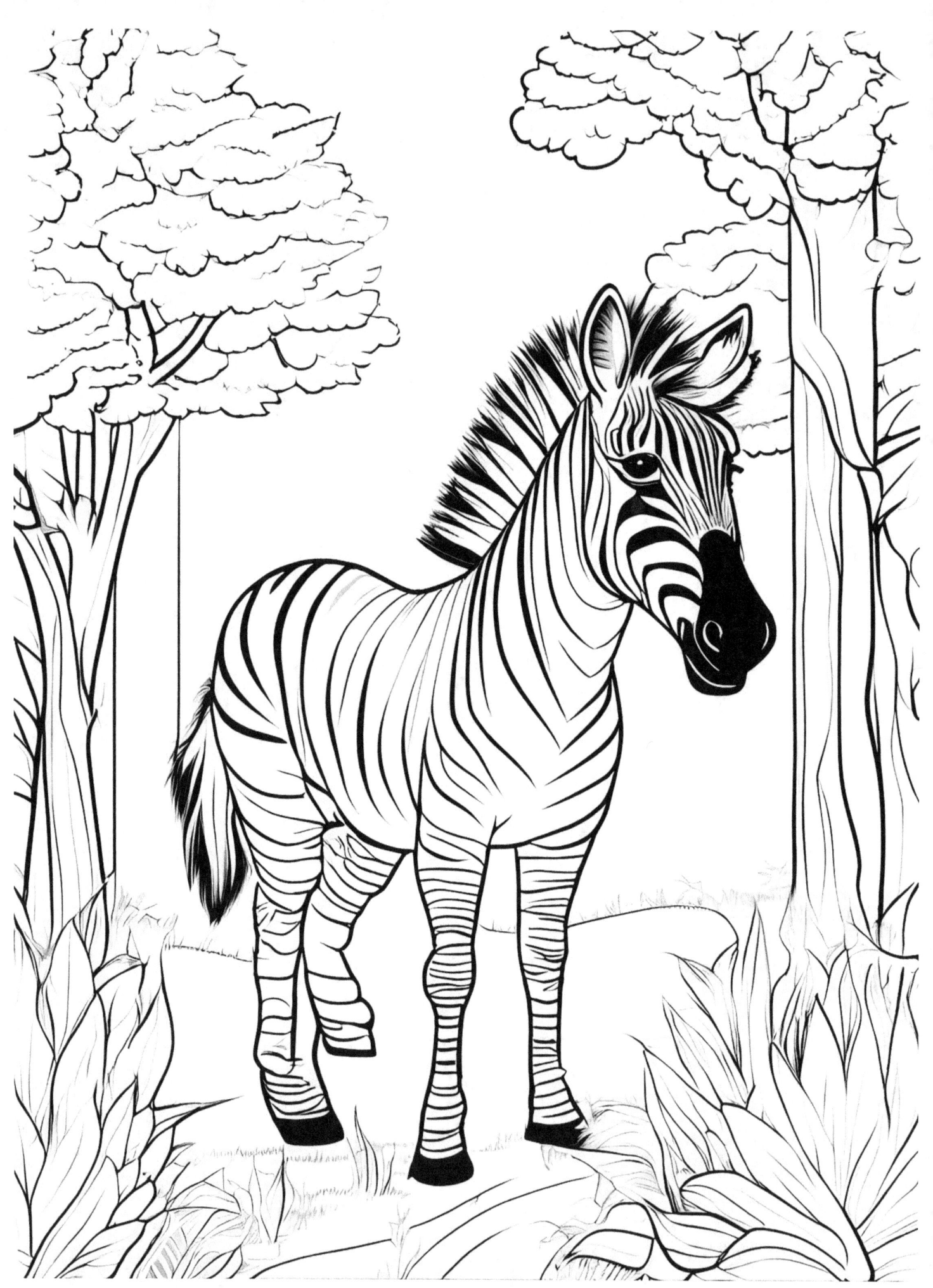

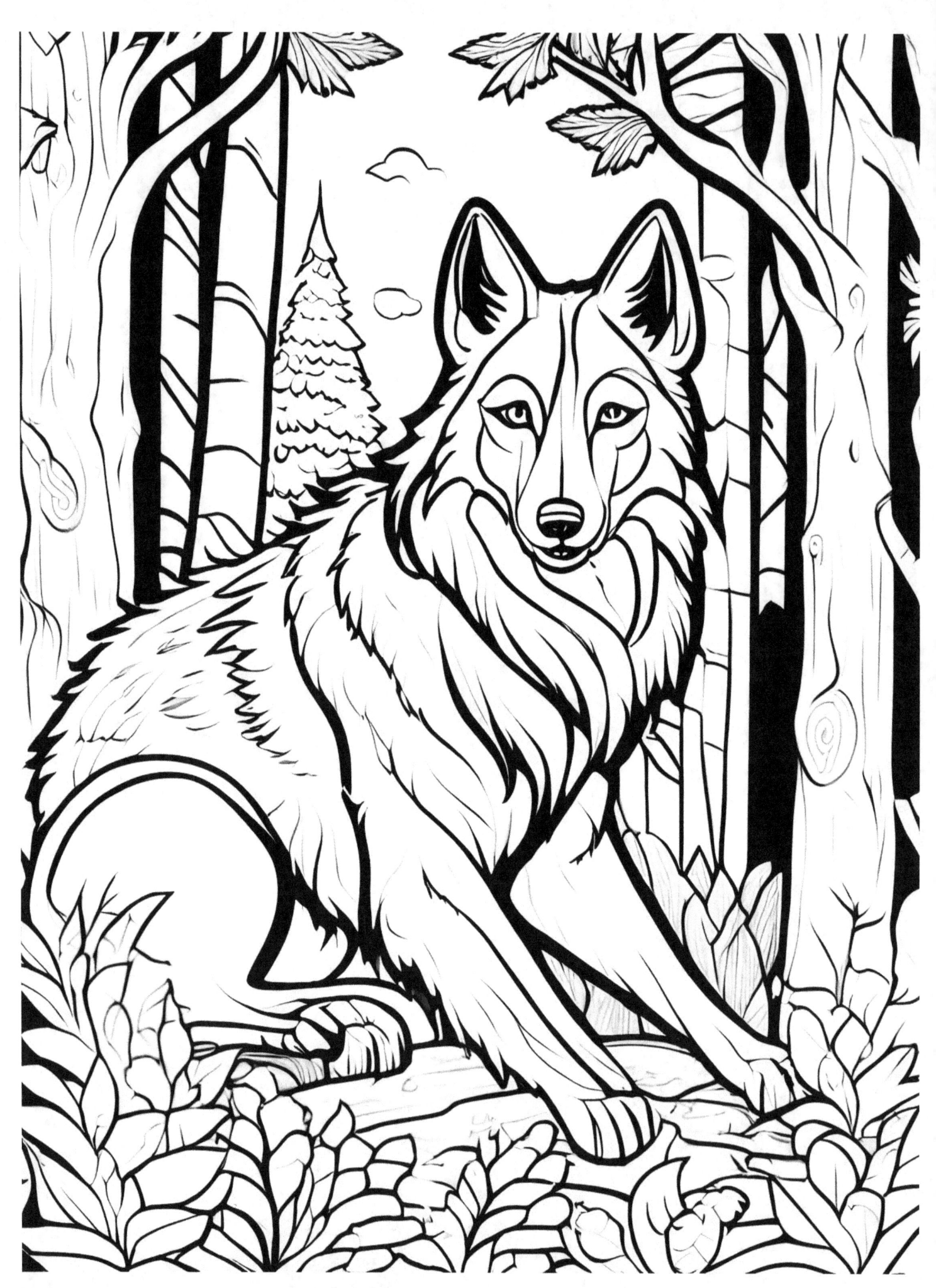

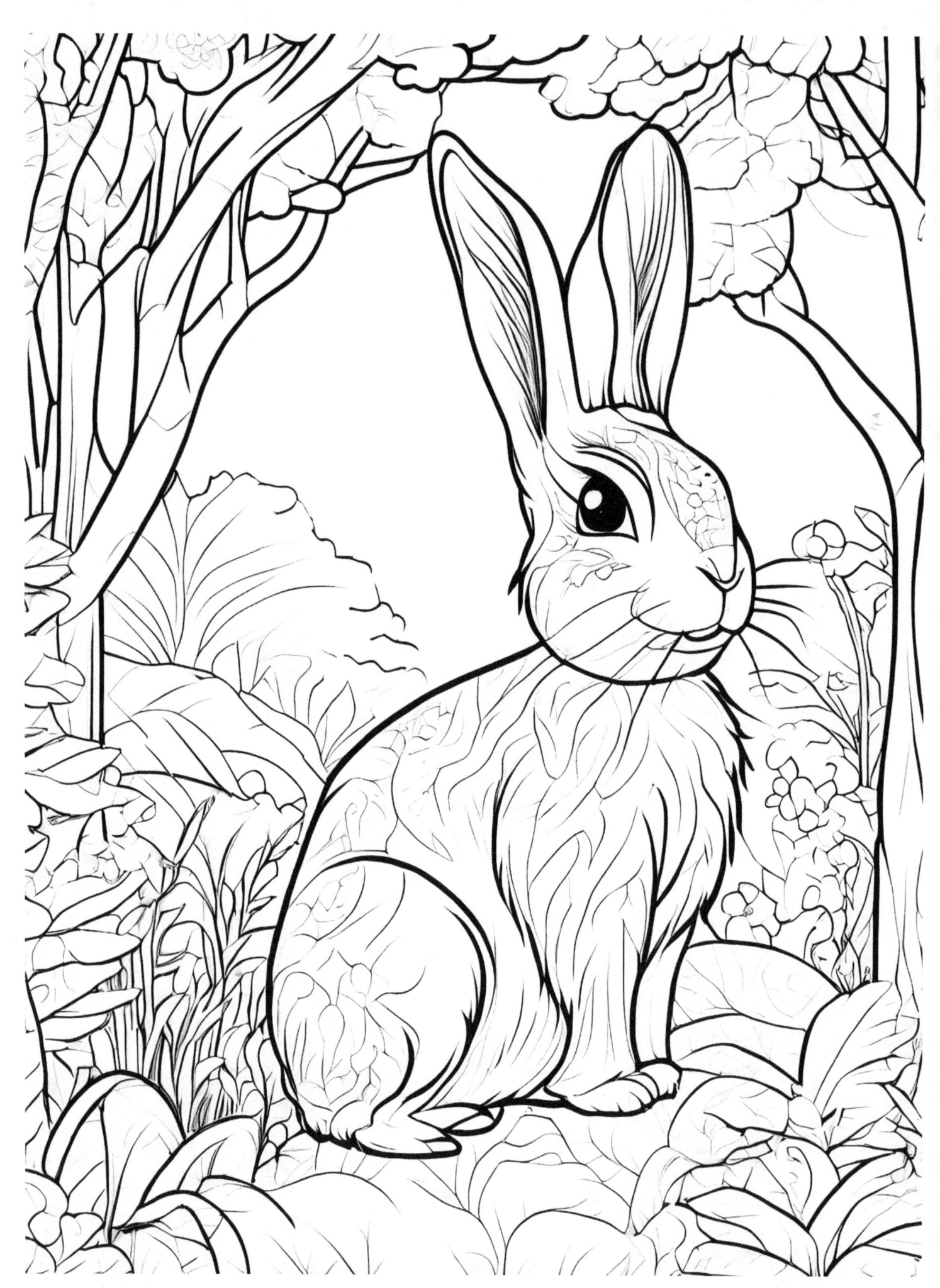

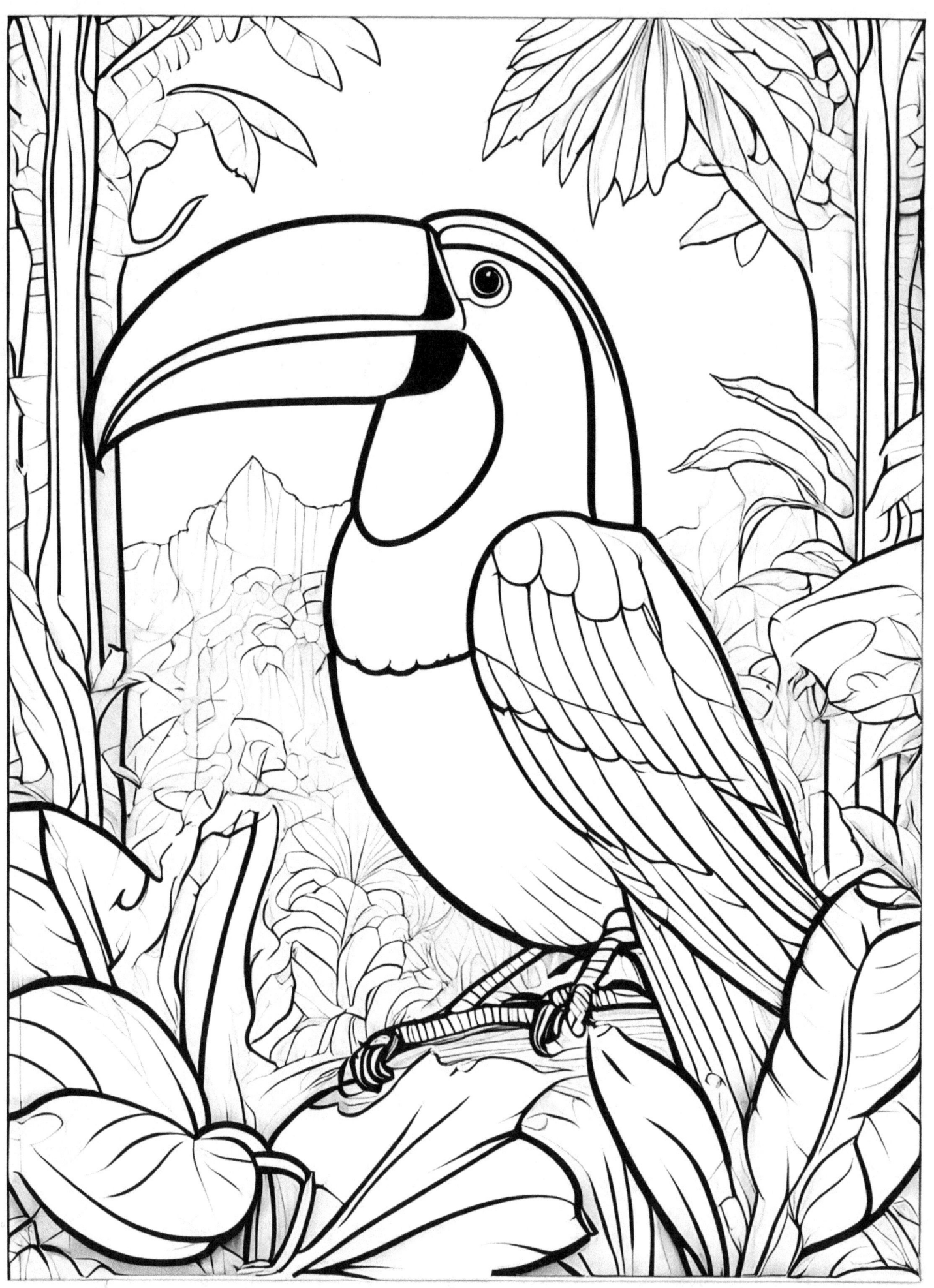

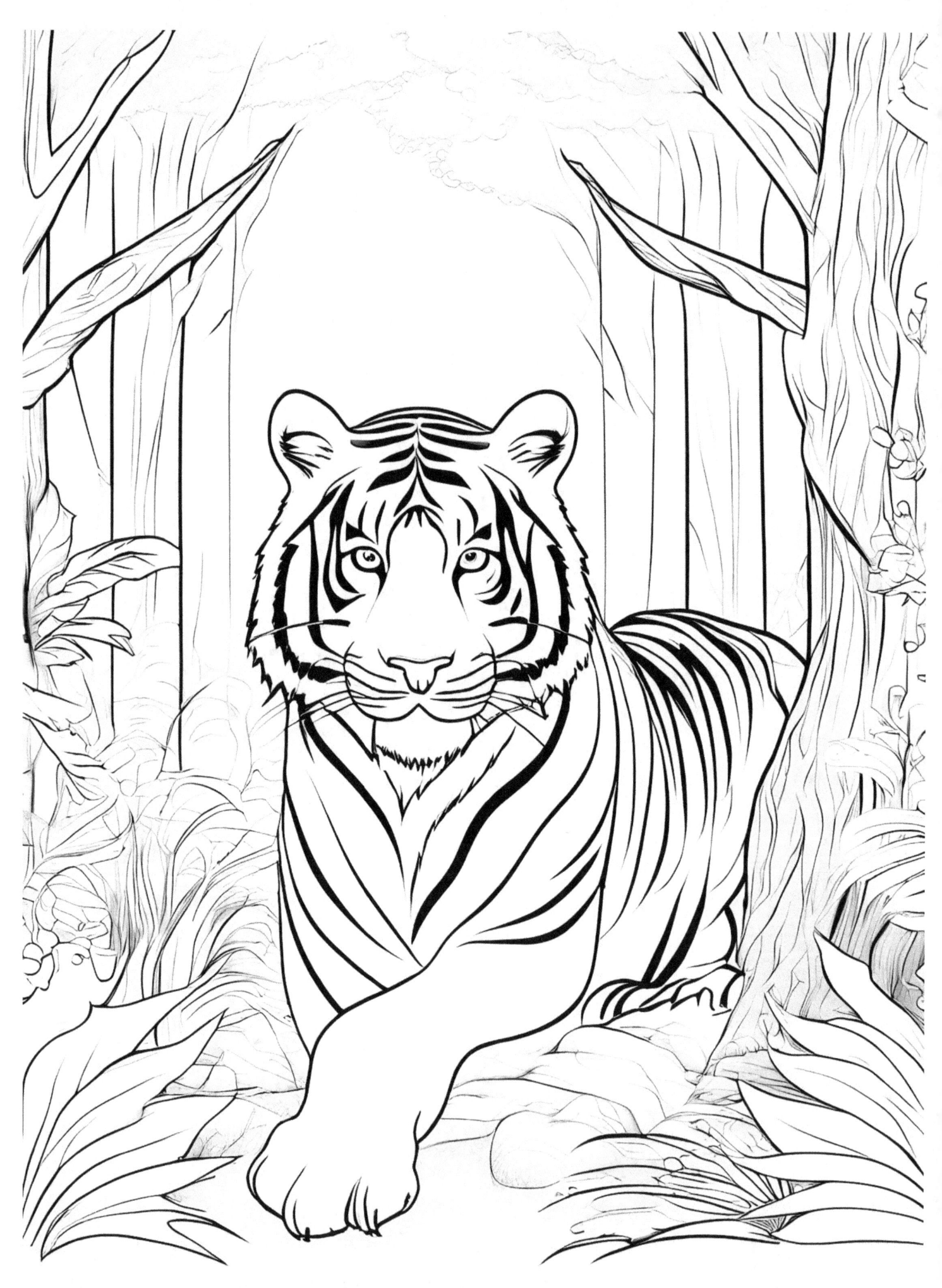

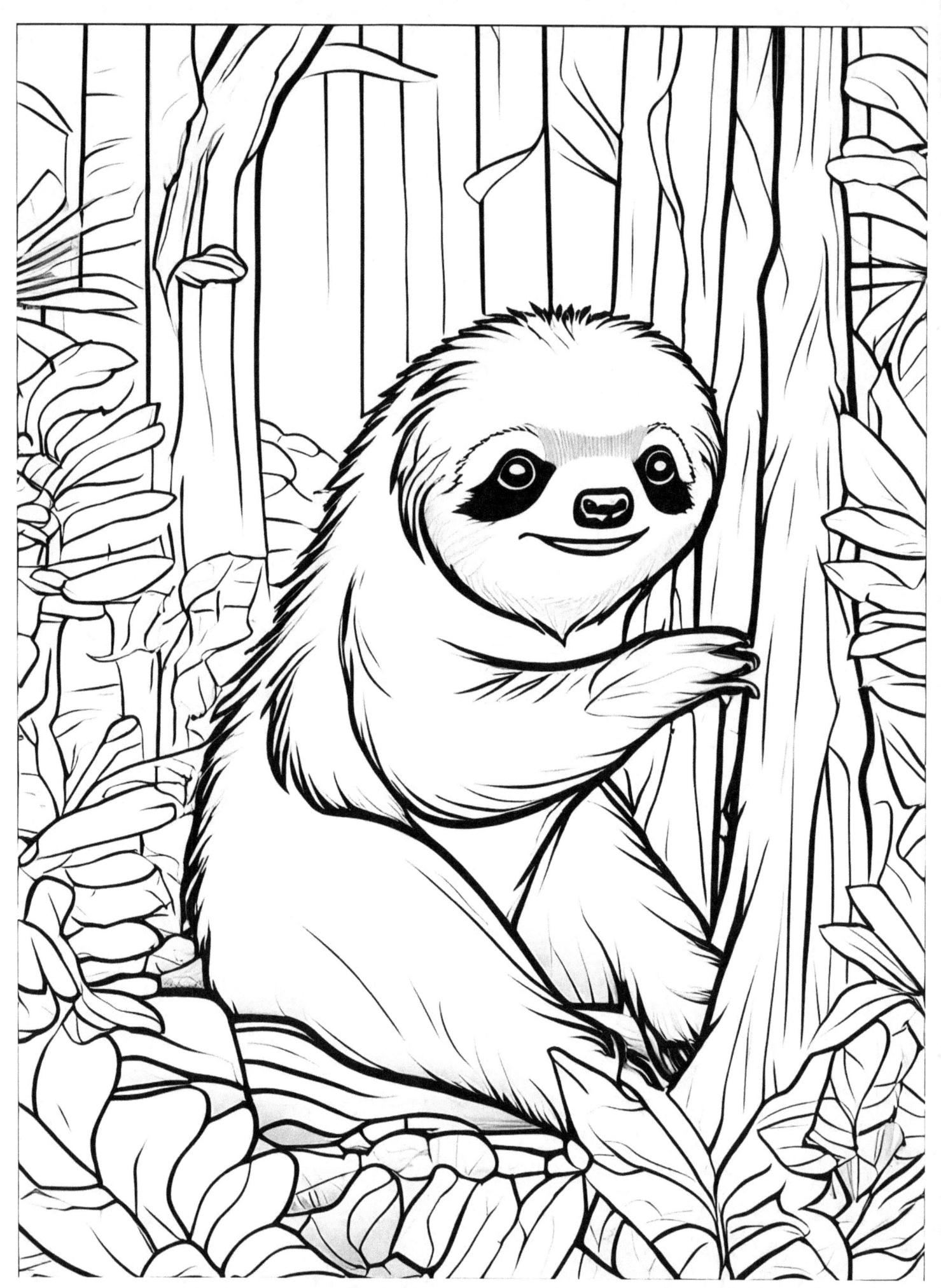

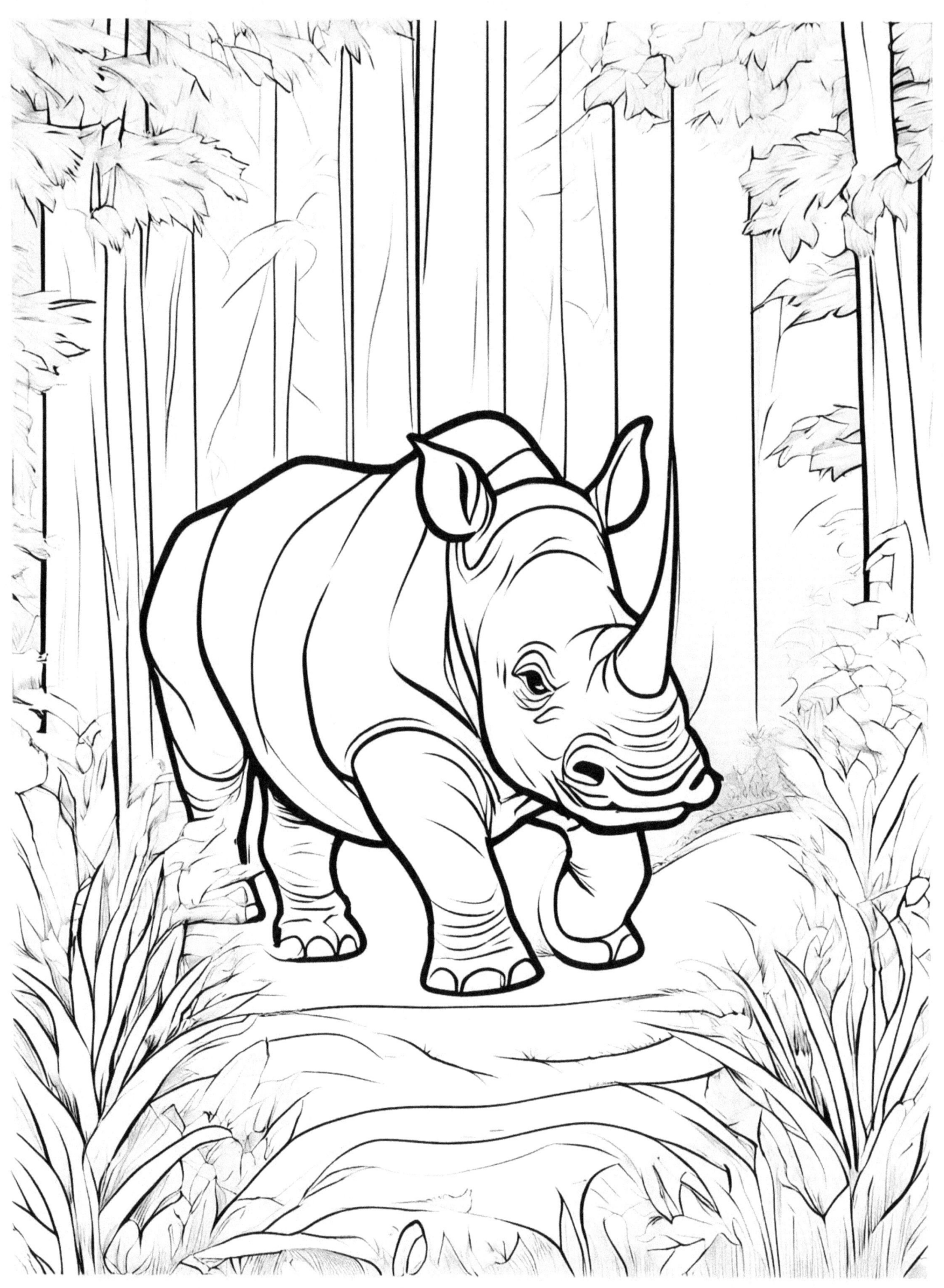

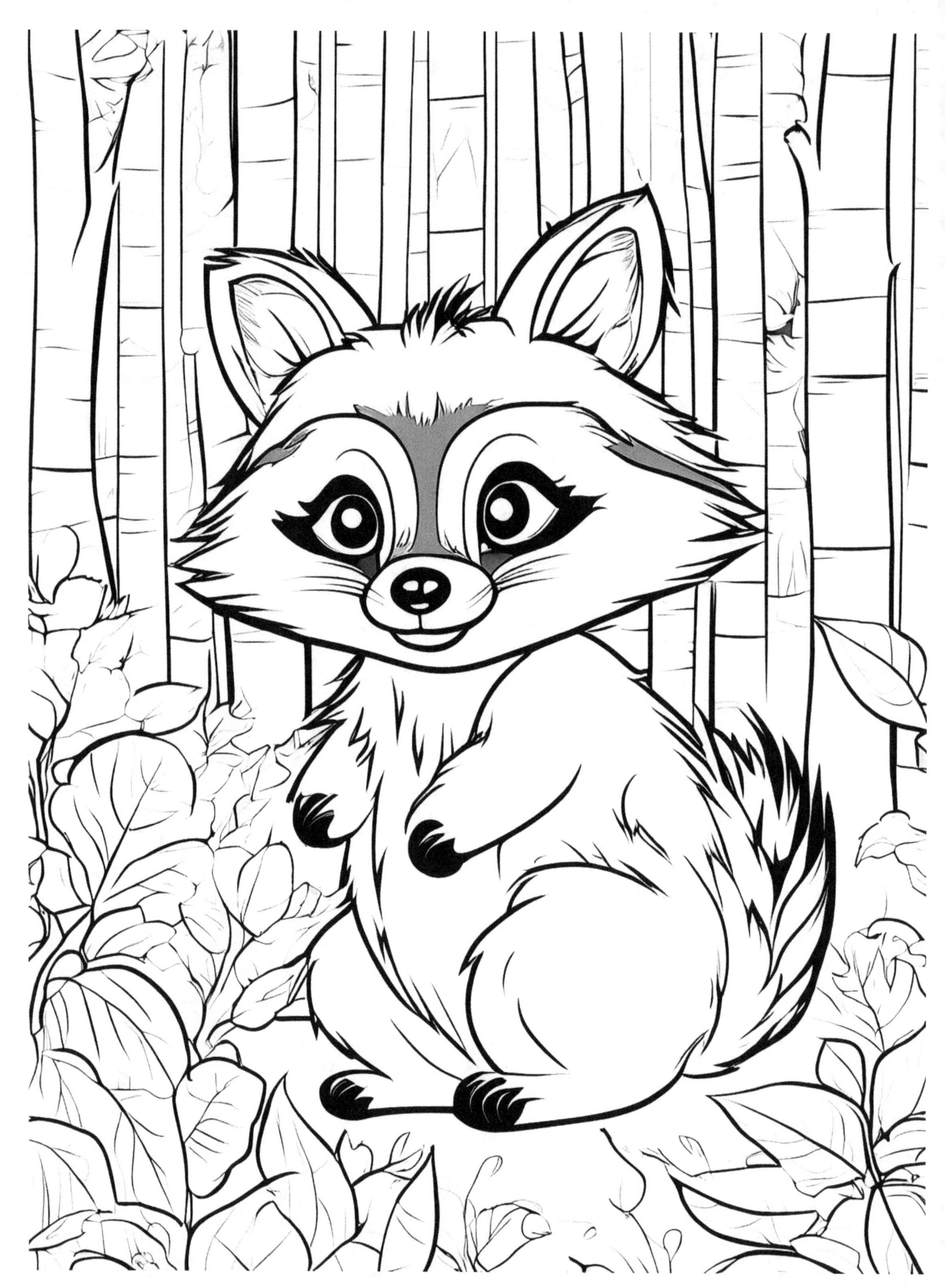

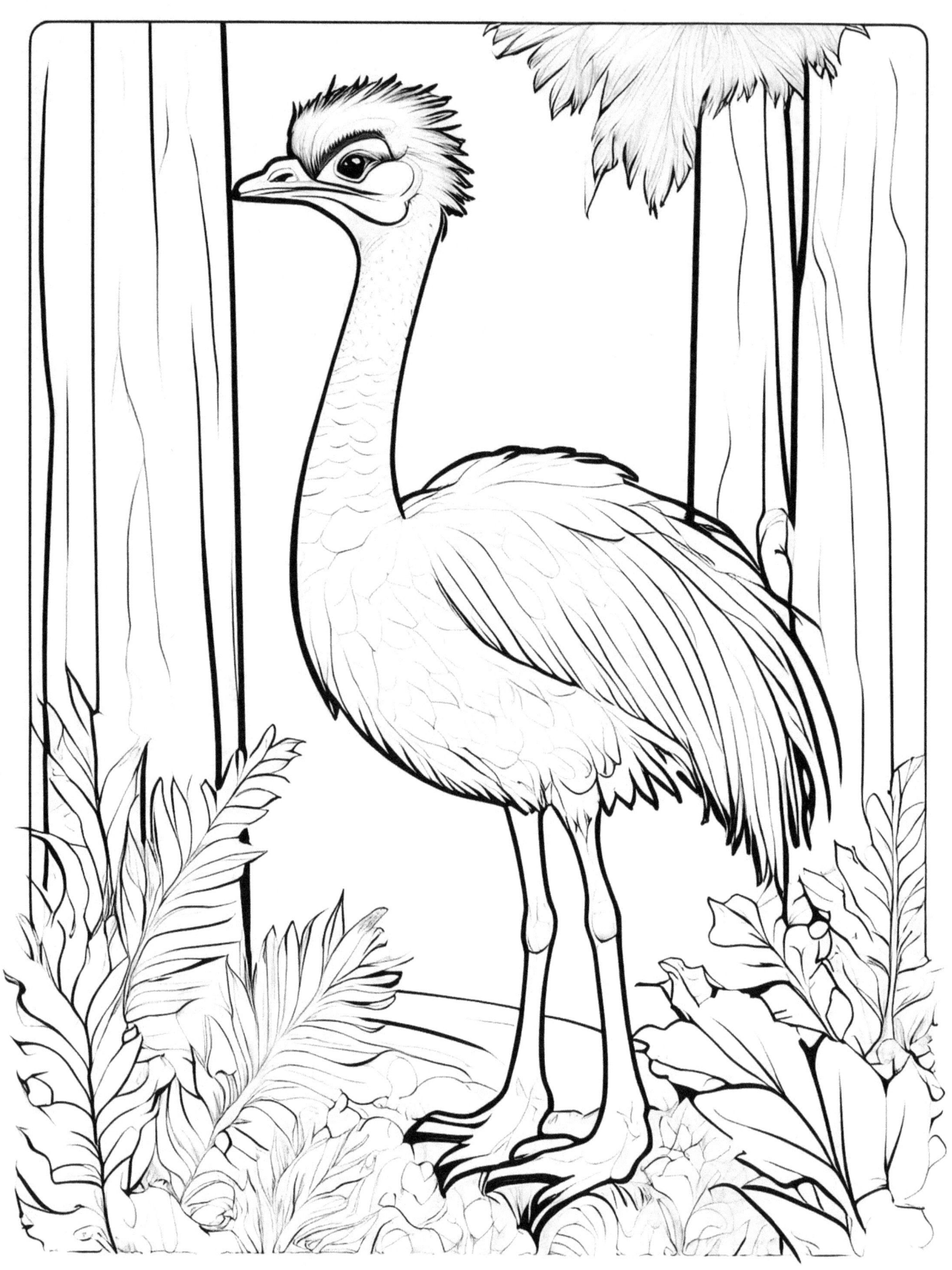

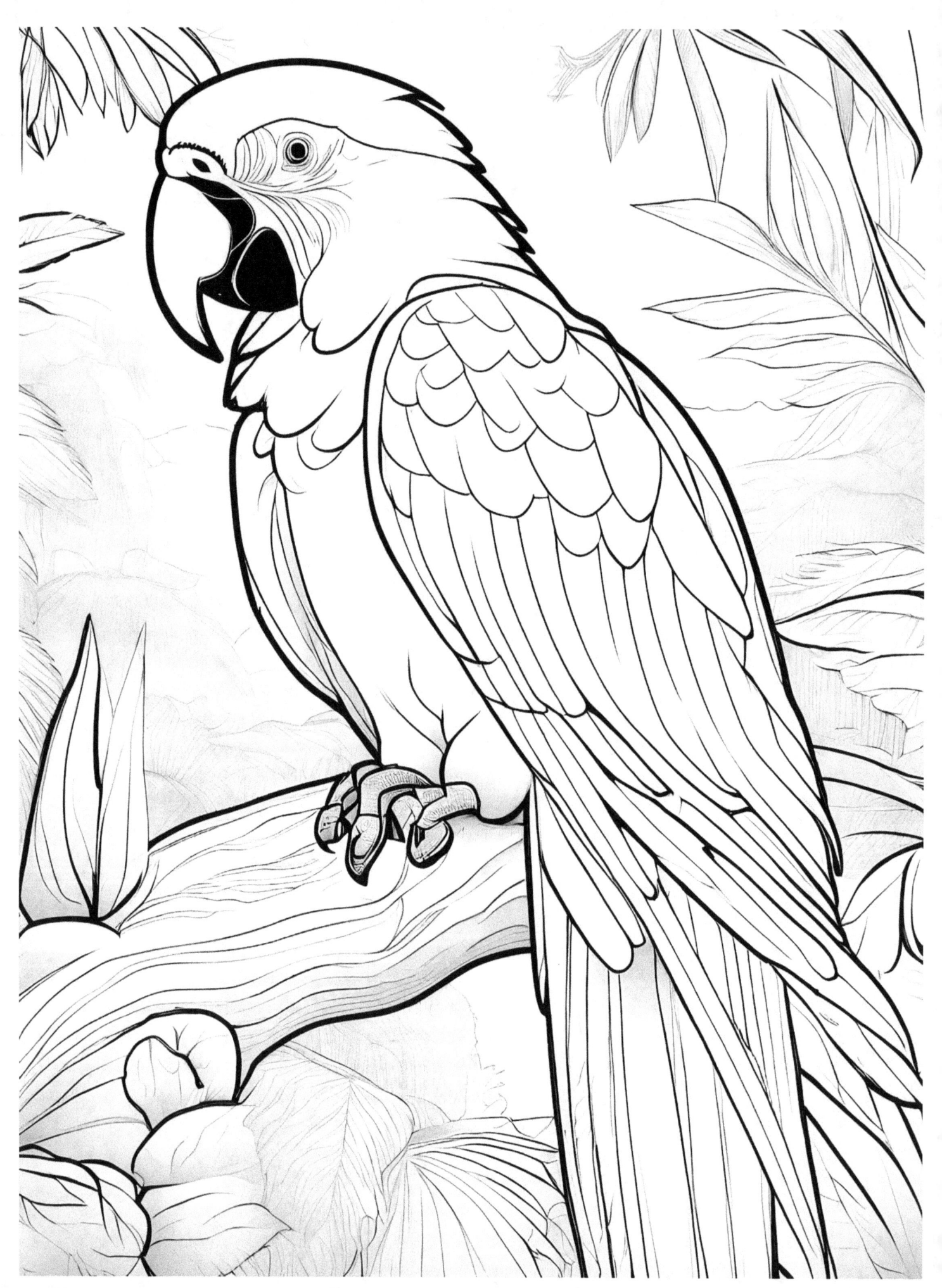

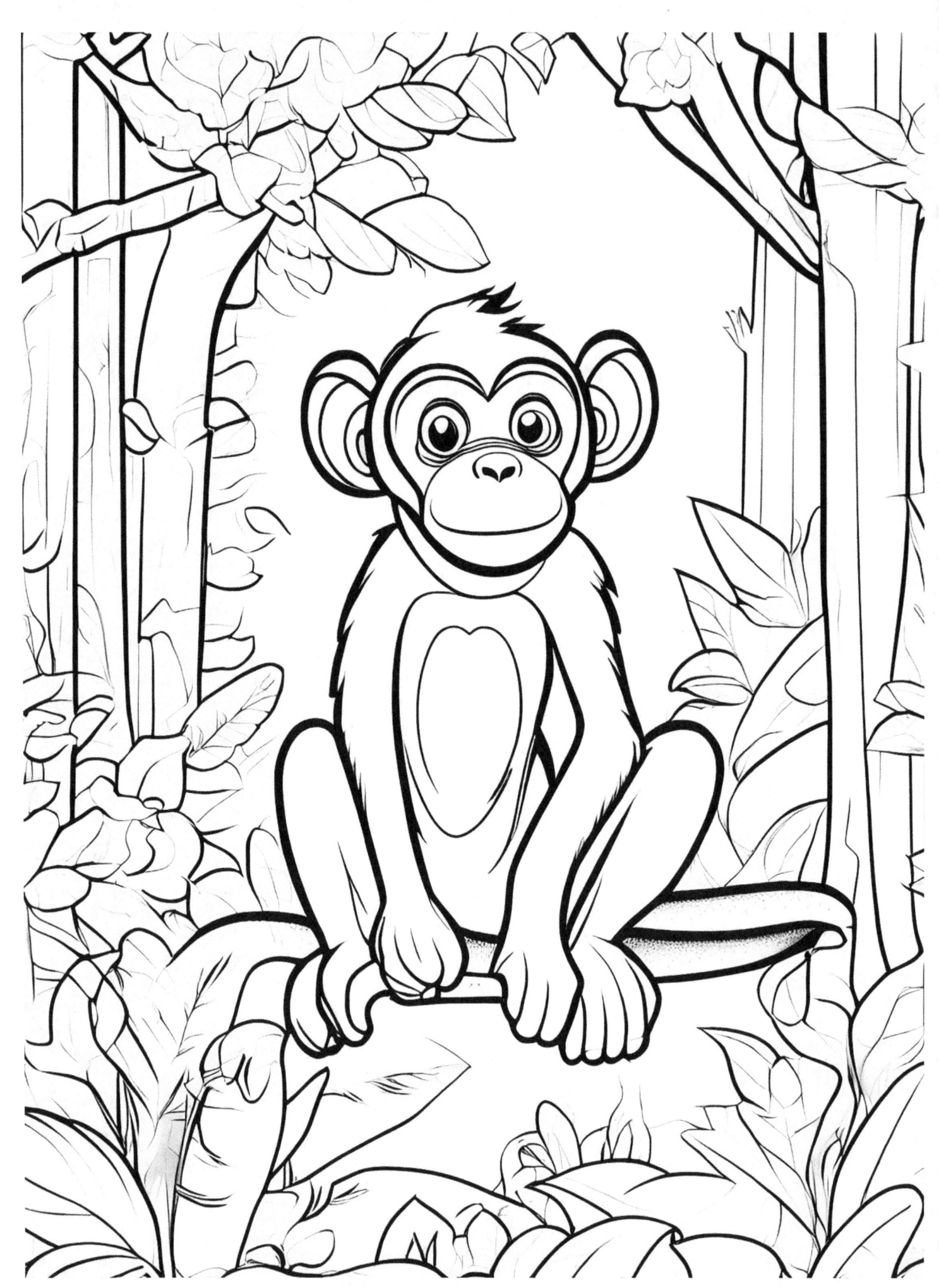

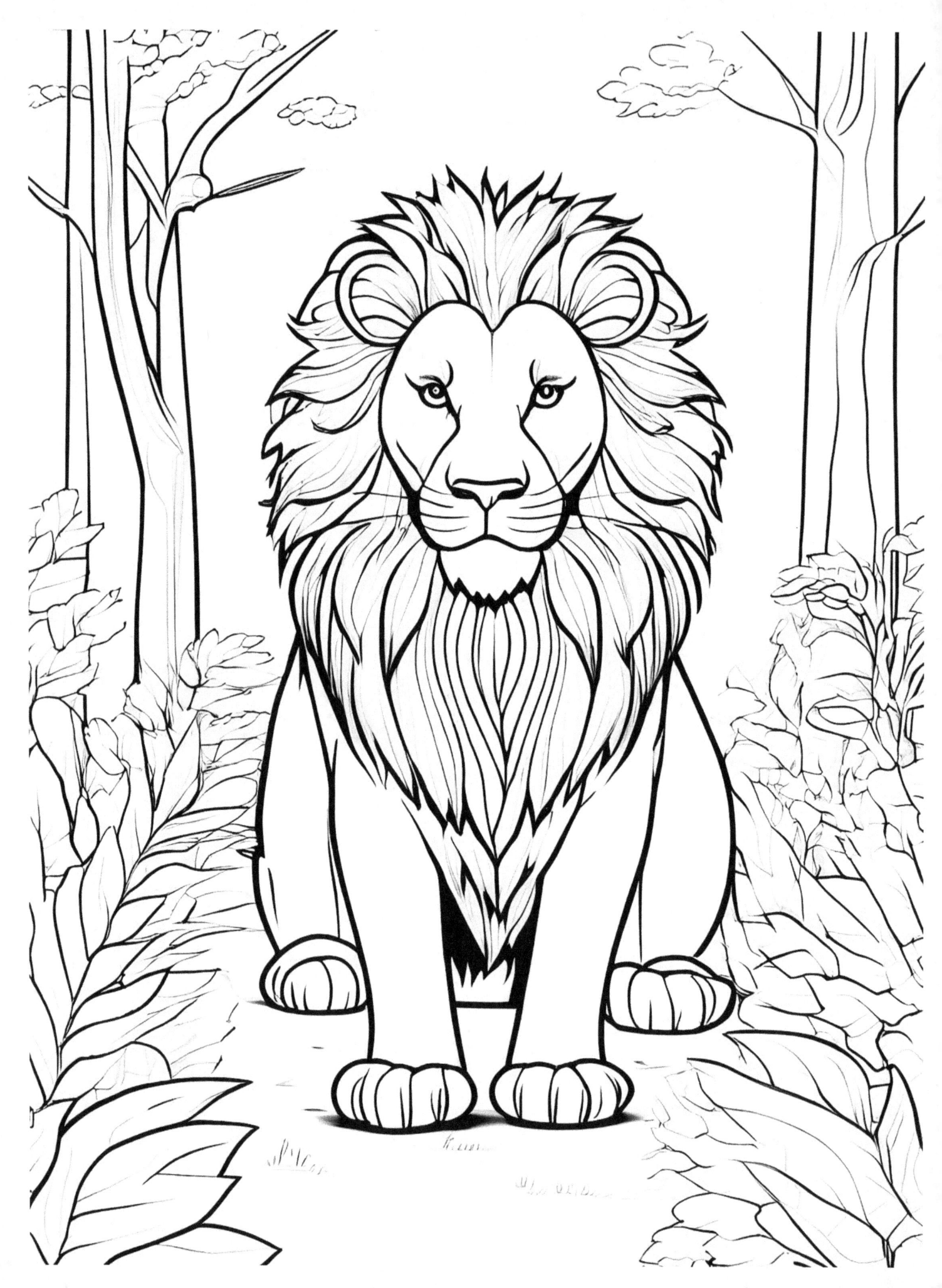

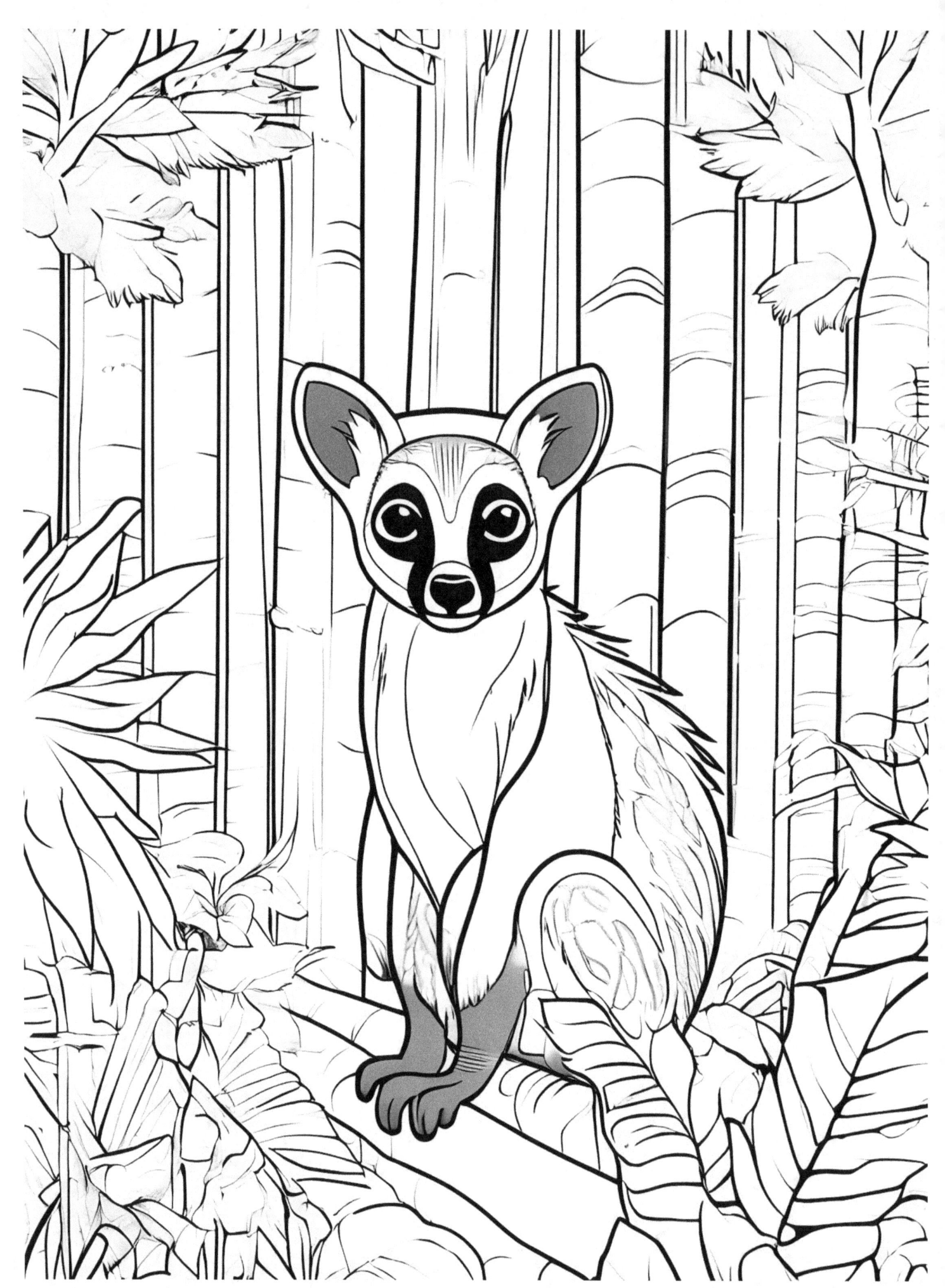

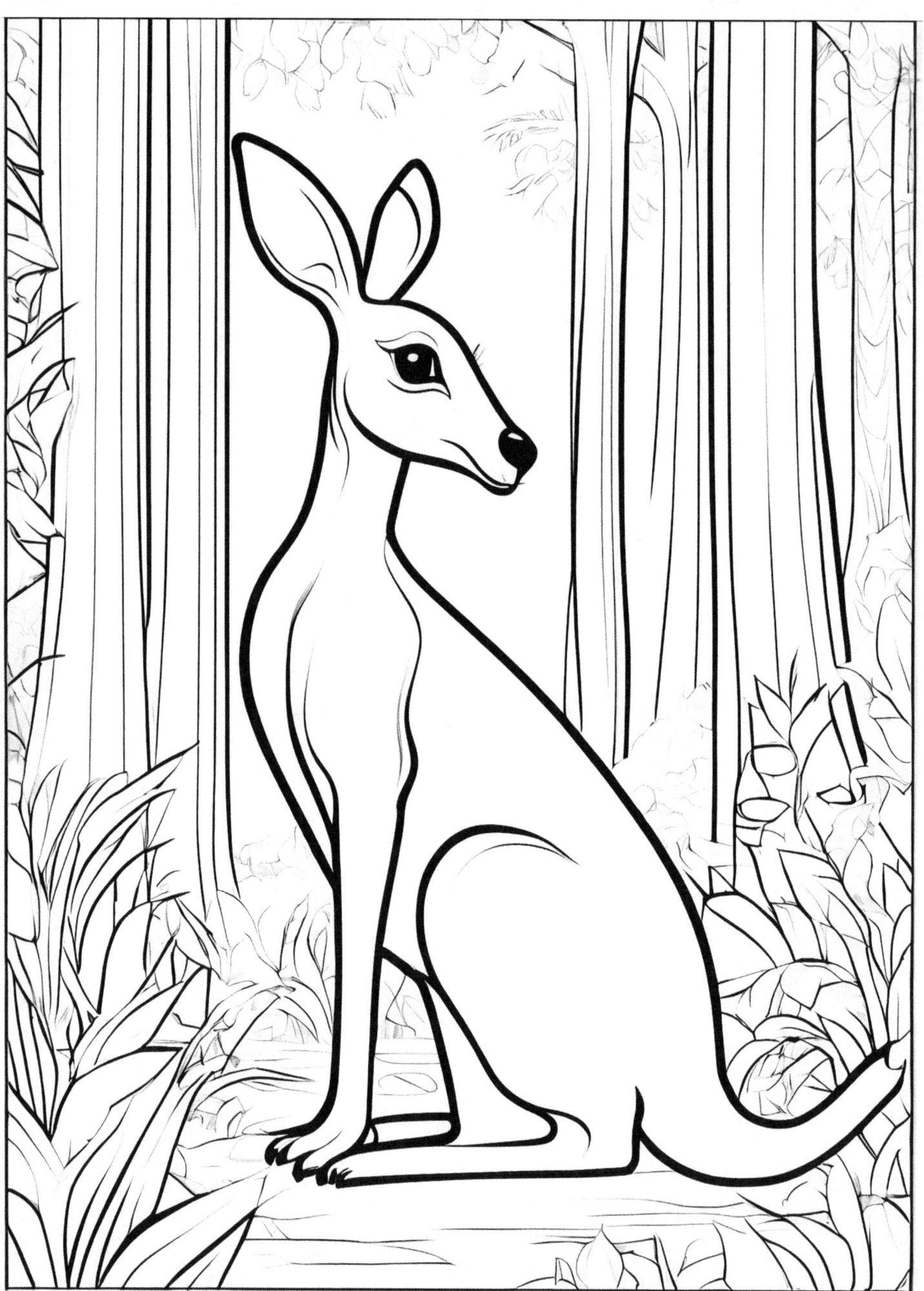

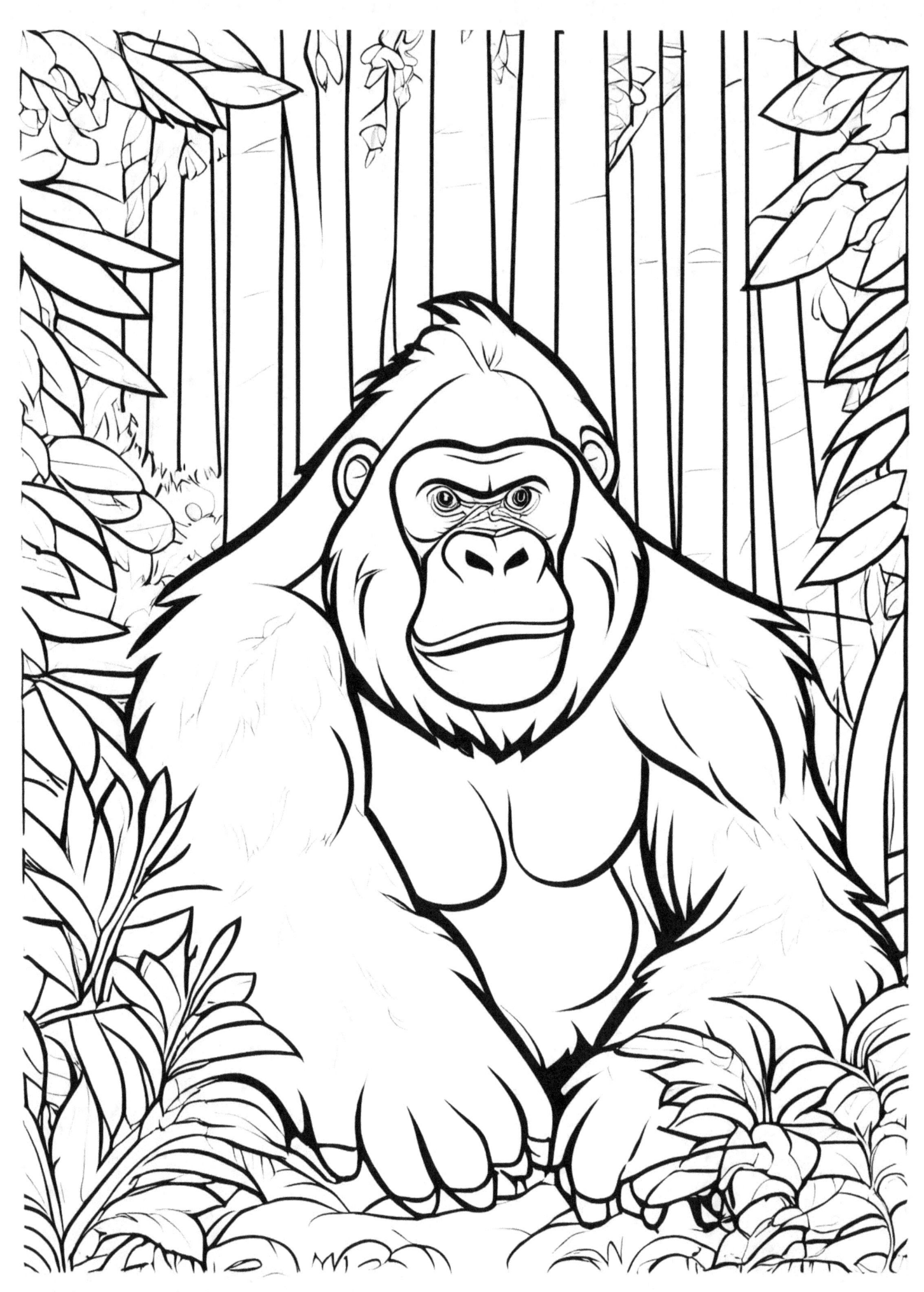

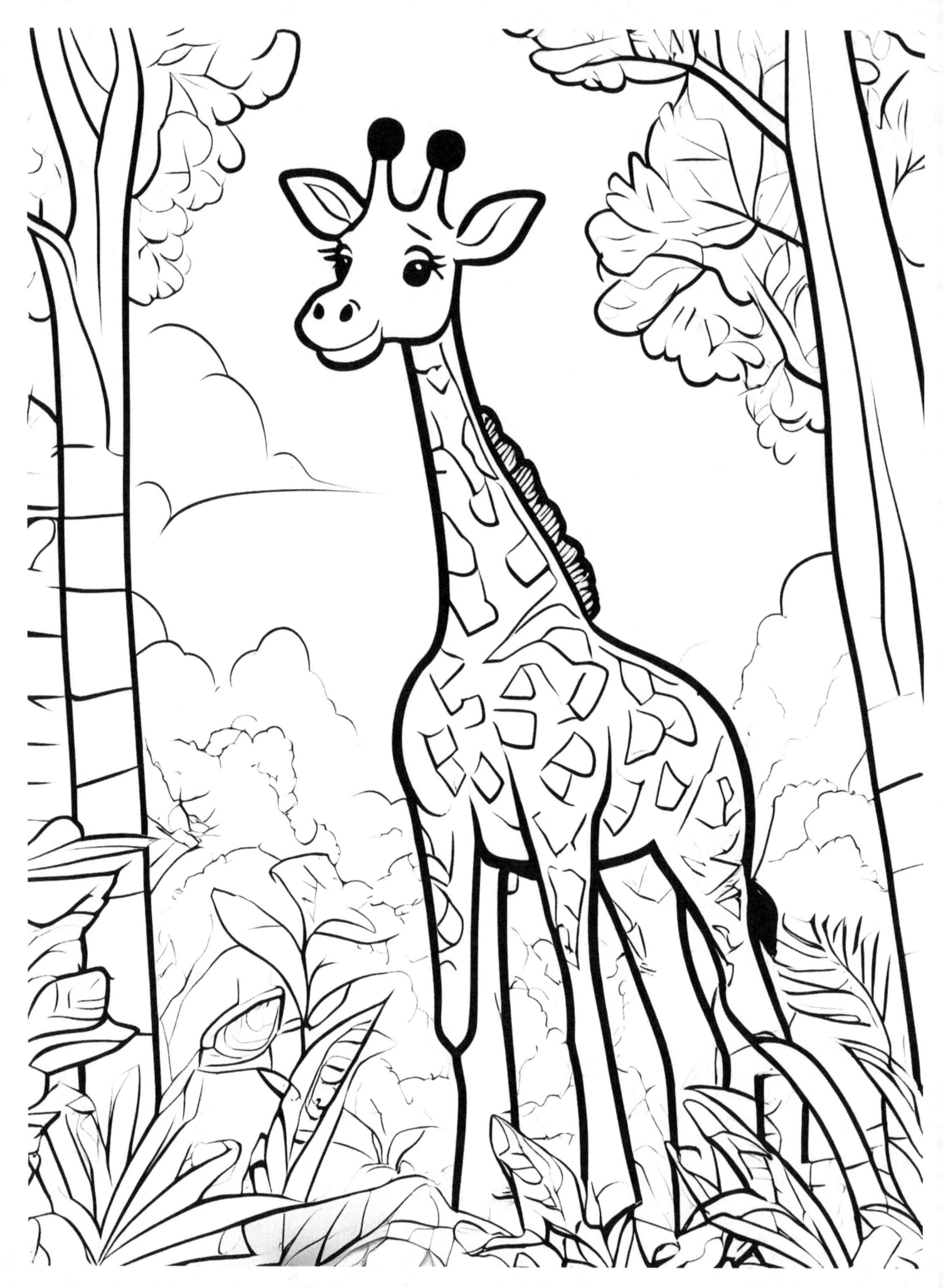

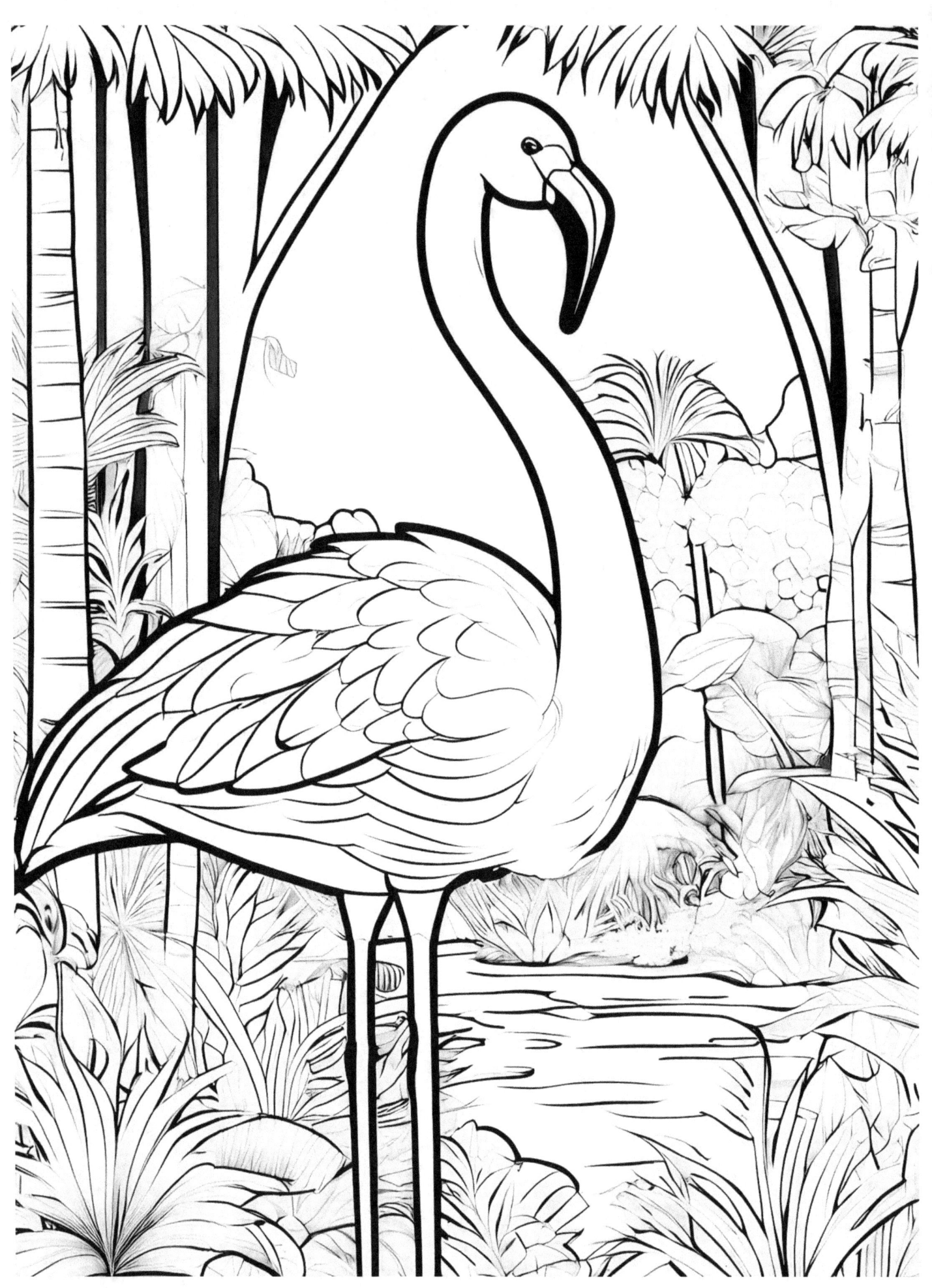

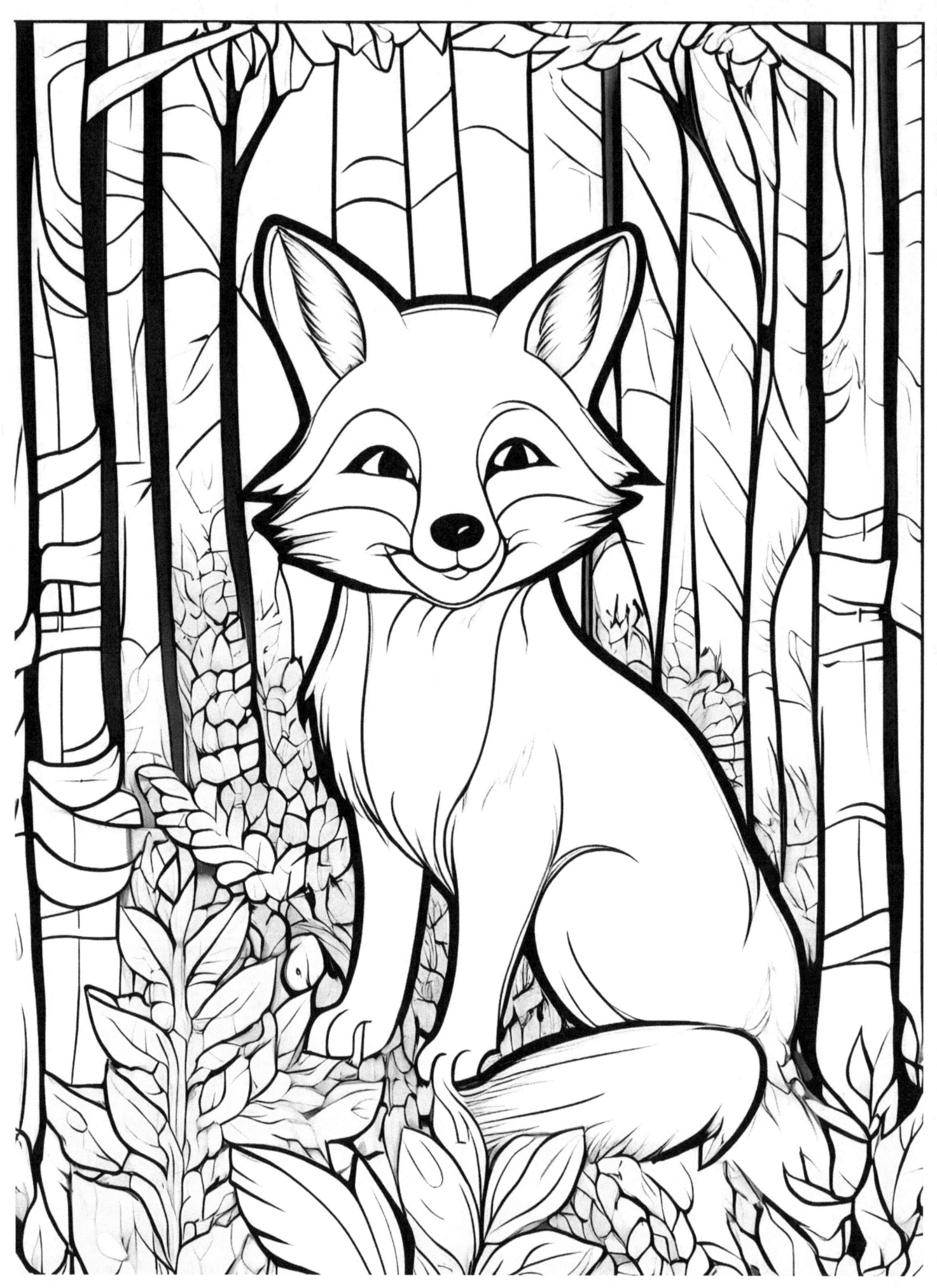

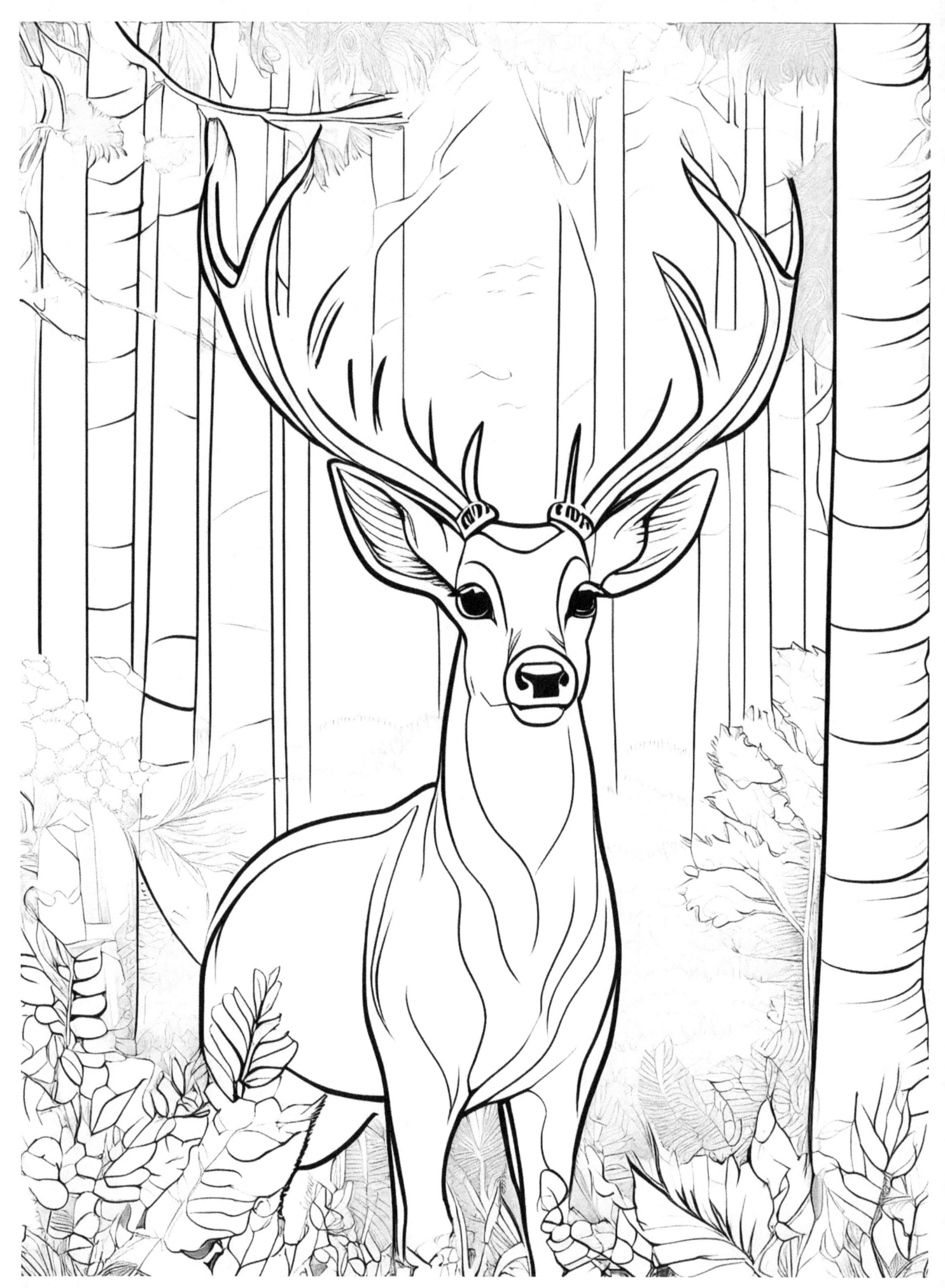

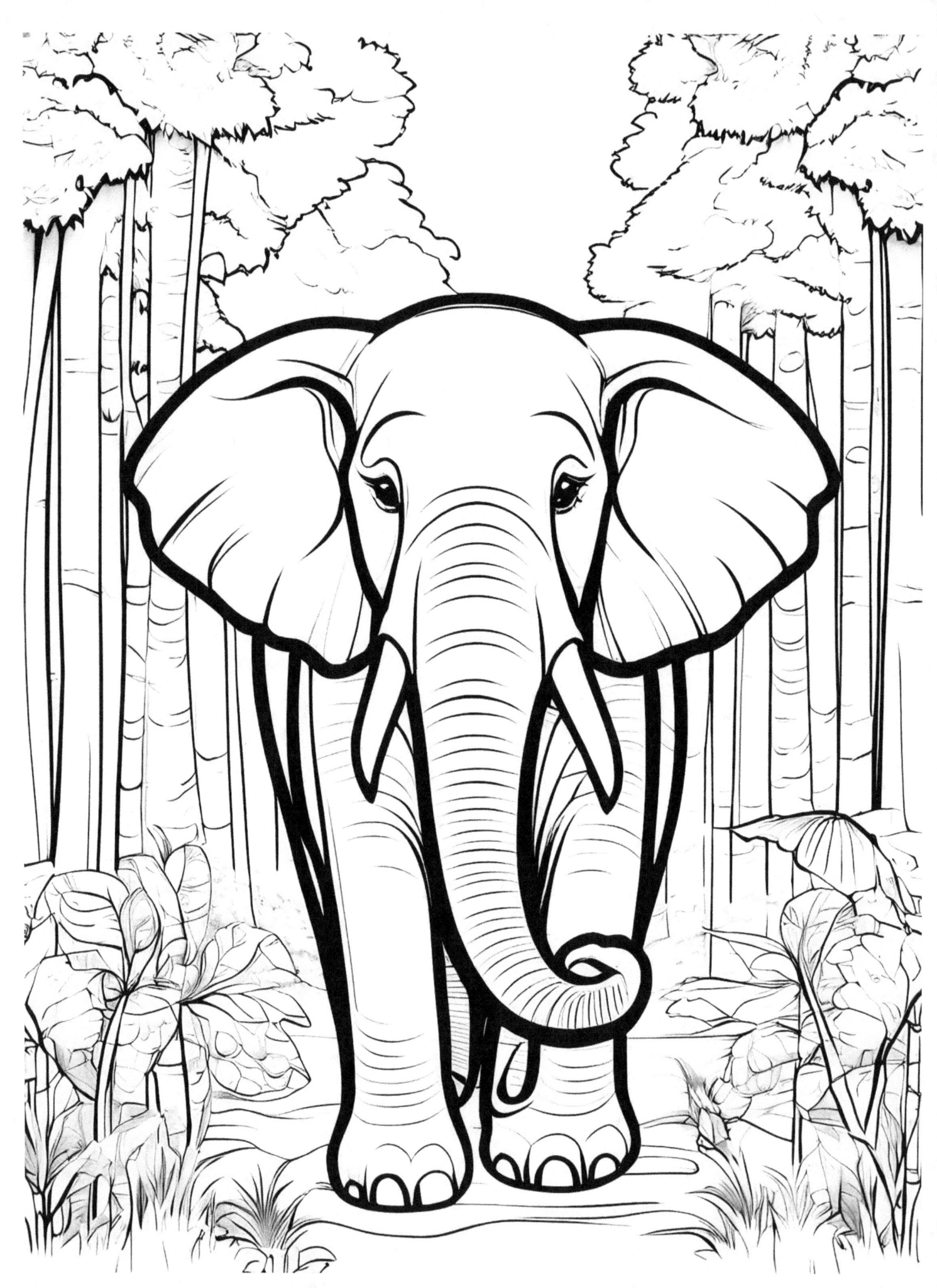

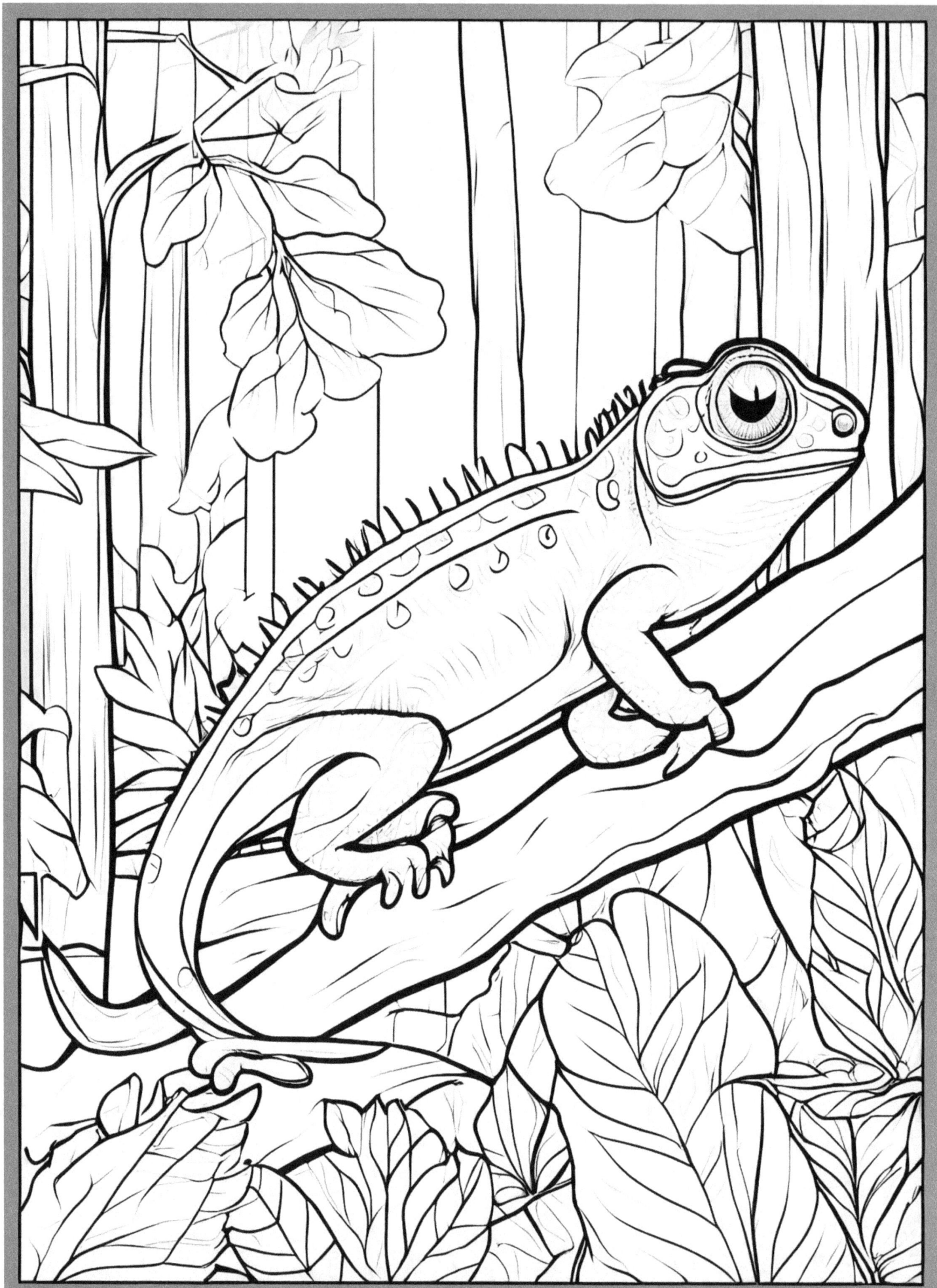

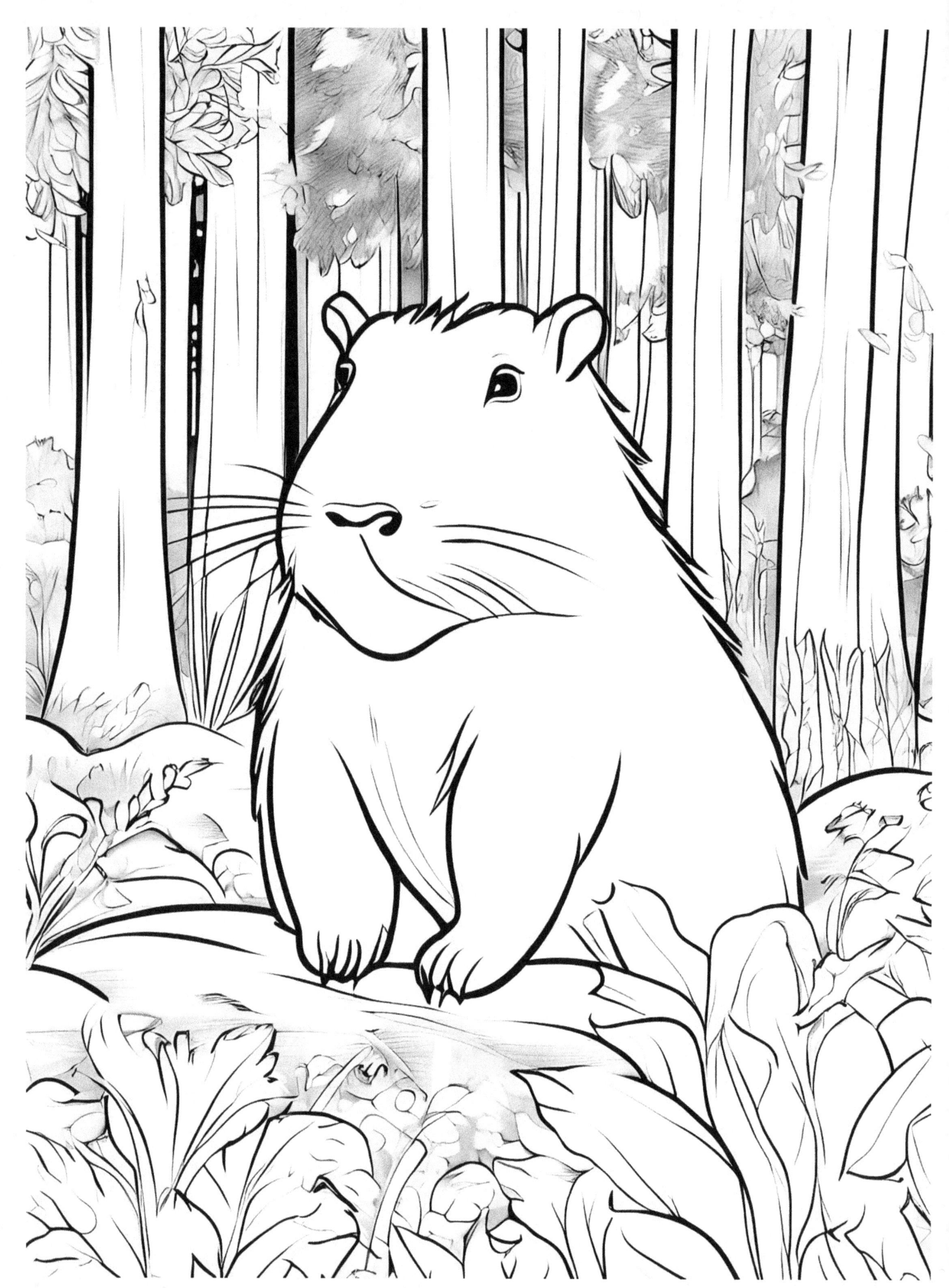

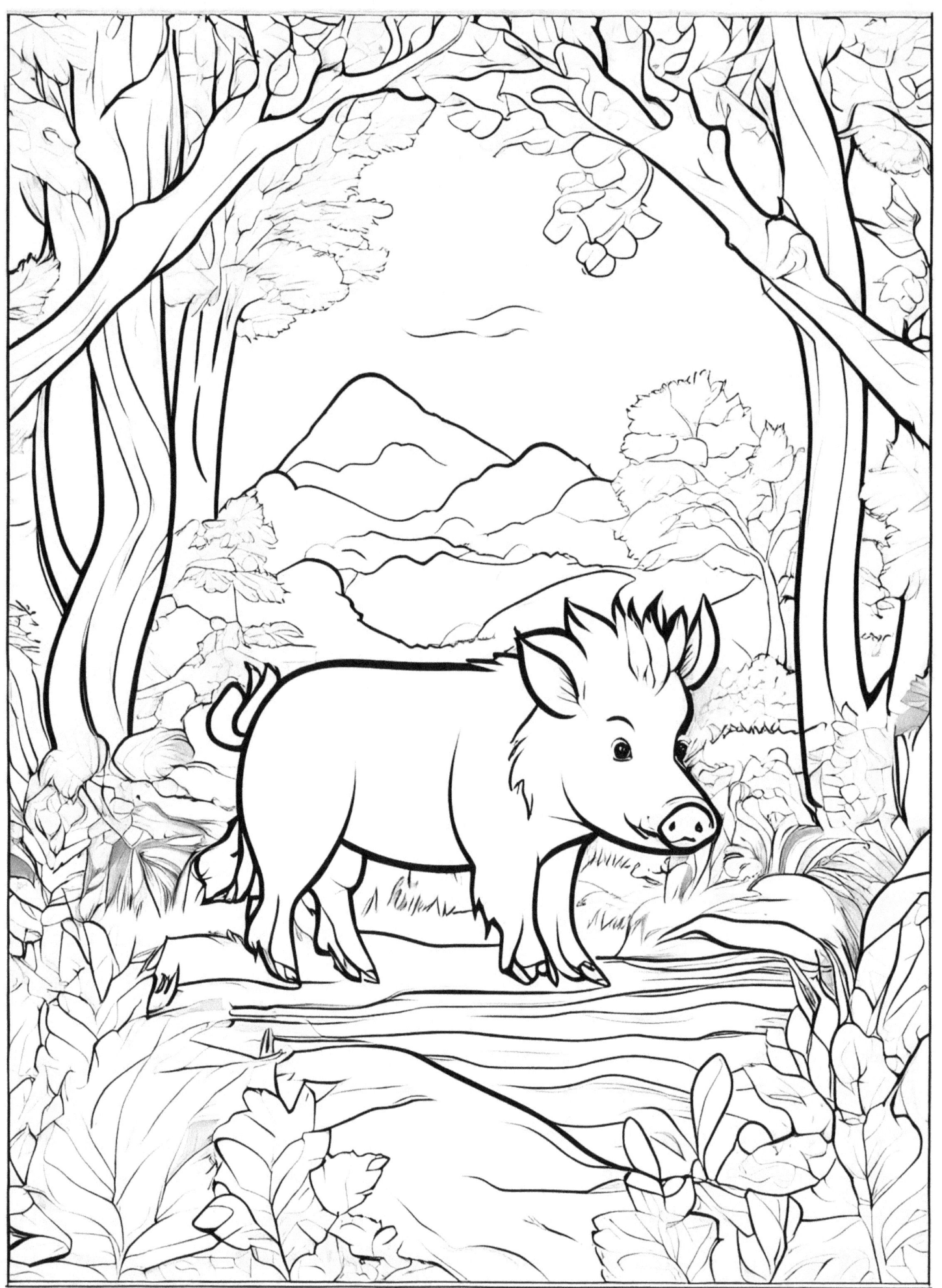

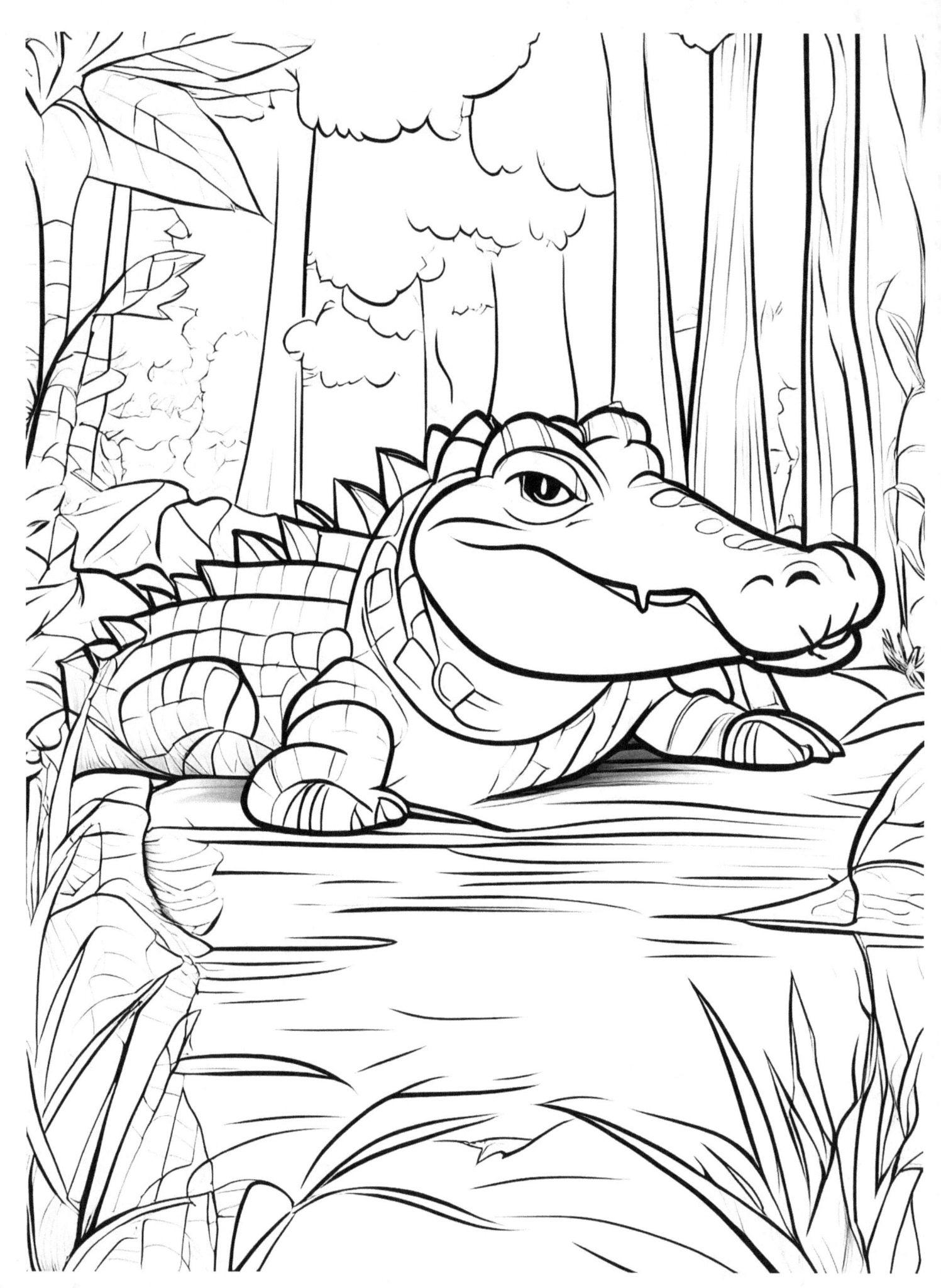

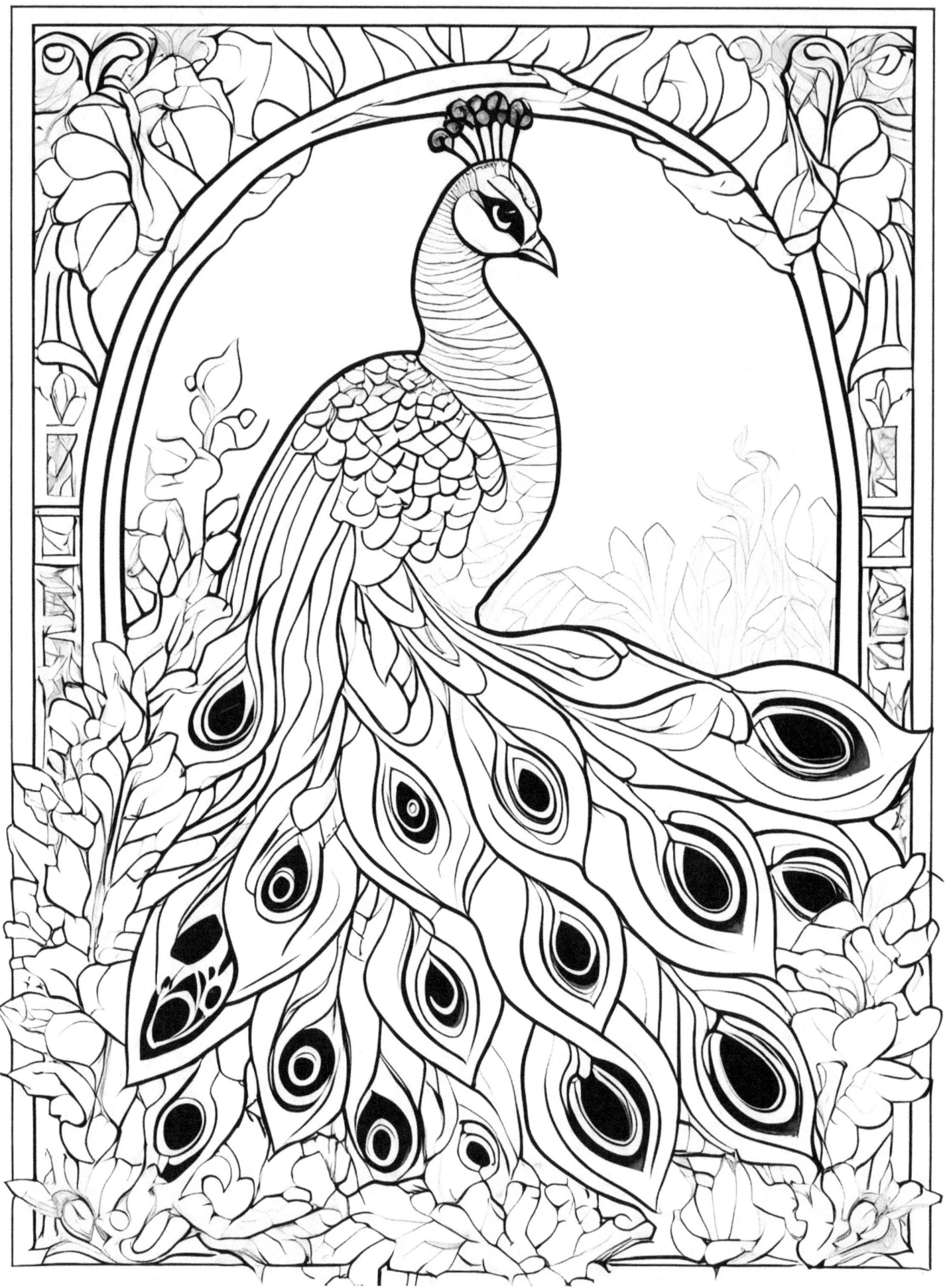